Science

AHEAD

Grade 6

Printed in China

Contents

Life Systems
1 Classification   5

Life Systems
2 Invertebrates   11

Life Systems
3 Vertebrates (1)   17

Life Systems
4 Vertebrates (2)   23

Matter and Materials
5 Properties of Air (1)   29

Review 1   35

Matter and Materials
6 Properties of Air (2)   41

Matter and Materials
7 Characteristics of Flight (1)   47

Matter and Materials
8 Characteristics of Flight (2)   53

Energy and Control
9 Static and Current Electricity (1)   59

Energy and Control
10 Static and Current Electricity (2) 65

Review 2 71

Energy and Control
11 More about Electricity 77

Structures and Mechanisms
12 Motion 83

Structures and Mechanisms
13 Motion and Machines 89

Earth and Space Systems
14 Earth and Our Solar System 95

Earth and Space Systems
15 The Night Sky 101

Review 3 107

Fun & Useful Facts 113

Answers 121

Classification

> Daddy, I don't want my lizard to catch a cold, so I've knitted him a sweater.

a cold-blooded animal

> You're so thoughtful, Tammy. But lizards are cold-blooded animals. They can regulate their body temperatures to match the temperatures of their surroundings.

In this unit, students will:

- sort living and non-living things into groups and put them in classification trees.
- classify animals as vertebrates or invertebrates.
- identify cold-blooded animals and warm-blooded animals.
- learn words related to vertebrates and invertebrates.

1

A. **Based on the characteristics of the given things, sort them into two groups and complete the classification trees.**

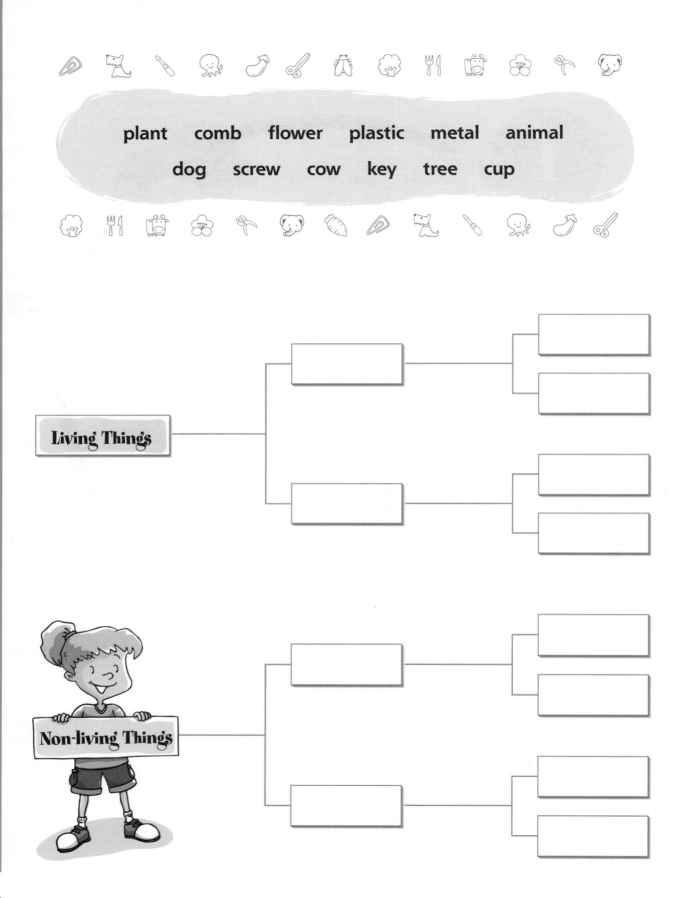

plant   comb   flower   plastic   metal   animal

dog   screw   cow   key   tree   cup

Living Things

Non-living Things

B. **Fill in the blanks to complete what Jimmy the Cat says. Then classify the animals by placing them in the correct boxes.**

We classify the 1._____ that make up the living world so that we

can understand and learn about them better. This classification is based on

the body 2._____ of the organisms.

The animal kingdom has many different types

of organisms. Animals without backbones are

called 3._____ . Animals with

backbones are called 4._____ .

> invertebrates
> organisms
> vertebrates
> structures

5.

cat   snail   turtle   squid

shark   centipede   grasshopper

snake   bird   earthworm

jellyfish   cheetah

Vertebrate

Invertebrate

1

C. Fill in the blanks to complete what the teacher says. Then tell whether each point is about a warm-blooded or cold-blooded creature. Write "warm-blooded" or "cold-blooded" on the line.

cold-blooded	temperature	warm-blooded

One of the ways to classify an animal is to look at the way it regulates or controls its body _____ .

A _____ animal's body temperature is the temperature of its surroundings. If the environment is hot, then it is hot as well. A _____ animal has the ability to keep its body at a constant temperature. It does this by having structural adaptations that allow it to change its body temperature from the inside.

Notes

1. converts food into energy to generate heat   _____

2. sweats   _____

3. burrows into soil to cool down   _____

4. generates heat by shivering   _____

5. flattens out body to let more sunlight hit
    its skin   _____

6. sheds hair in the summer to cool down   _____

7. changes skin colour to absorb more heat
    from the sun   _____

D. The words below all have something to do with vertebrates or invertebrates. Find them out and circle them.

Vertebrates

amphibians   reptiles

mammals   fish   birds

gills   milk

Invertebrates

exoskeleton   thorax   centipedes

arthropod   insects   worms

sponges   mollusks

a	b	a	r	e	p	t	i	l	e	s	m	n	k	j
c	t	m	a	m	m	a	l	s	x	p	o	b	e	x
e	w	p	q	t			t	o	d	m	i	l	k
n	a	h	y	n			h	s	f	o	r	a	u
t	f	i	s	h	s	z	f	o	k	s	l	d	d
i	t	b	g	o	p	u	r	r	e	y	l	s	g	m
p	s	i	x	u	o	p	w	a	l	k	u	h	a	s
e	s	a			n	e	y	x	e	a	s	g	l	g
d	w	n		g	z	n	a	t	h	k	i
e	j	s	b	o	e			o	f	s	l
s	w	o	r	m	s			n	w	j	l	v	r
					i	n	s	e	c	t	s	n	w
m	i	l	q	a	r	t	h	r	o	p	o	d	a	d

9

1

My Own Classification

Materials:

- a box of 50 assorted buttons
- a timer

Classification means the objects are sorted and put in a specific place.

You can sort the buttons by their colour.

buttons

Steps:

1. Give a player the assorted buttons.

2. Ask the player to choose any one of the characteristics, such as size, colour, texture, number of holes, and shape to group the buttons.

3. Time the player and record the time taken.

4. Ask the next player to regroup the buttons based on a different characteristic.

5. Time the second player and record the time taken.

6. Repeat the steps for each player.

7. The fastest one to finish the grouping is the winner.

Player	Time Taken

Are you able to...

- [ ] sort living and non-living things into groups and put them in classification trees?
- [ ] classify animals as vertebrates or invertebrates?
- [ ] identify cold-blooded animals and warm-blooded animals?
- [ ] find words related to vertebrates and invertebrates?

Invertebrates

Welcome to the world of **Invertebrates**

I'm an octopus. I'm an invertebrate and under the group of mollusks. All the animals under this group have soft-bodies or live in hard shells. My friends, oysters and clams, are also under this group.

In this unit, students will:

- name some invertebrates.
- match invertebrates with the correct descriptions.
- describe and identify insects.
- answer questions related to insects.

2

A.   Look at the pictures of invertebrates. Name them.

worms   sponges   sand dollars
arthropods   mollusks   sea anemones

1.

_____

2.

_____

3.

_____

4.

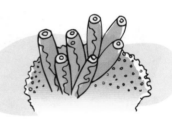

_____

5.

6.

B. **Match the descriptions with the pictures of invertebrates on the previous page. Write the names of the invertebrates on the lines. Then sort the animals. Write the letters.**

1. _____ ◯ :

   flat, round, and segmented – the earthworm is highly developed in its organ systems

2. _____ ◯ :

   tough, jointed exoskeleton; segmented body; the most successful animal on the planet; found anywhere there is land; includes insects

3. _____ ◯ :

   have a one- or two-part shell; some have a muscular foot that they use with slime to move upon

4. _____ ◯ :

   ocean dwellers; have rays or arms; a water-filled canal system and tube feet that allow for movement

5. _____ ◯ :

   tube-shaped body; different cells do different jobs; filter feeders; water flows through bodies; certain cells filter out food

6. _____ ◯ :

   simple bag within a bag body design; two cell layers; stinging cells on tentacles

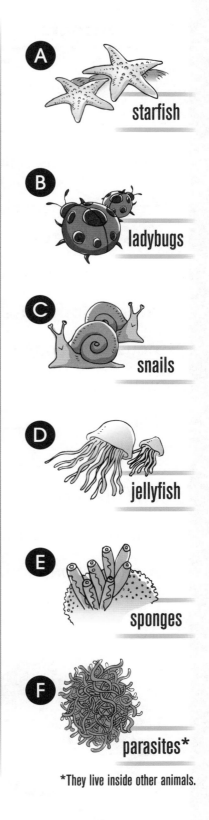

A starfish

B ladybugs

C snails

D jellyfish

E sponges

F parasites*

*They live inside other animals.

2

C. Fill in the blanks with the given words. Then identify the insect in each group. Circle it.

Insects

adaptations
exoskeleton
thorax
sound
arthropods
circulation
three
sense
legs

Insects belong to the phylum arthropod, the

1. _____ . They are the most diverse

and numerous animals in the world. They have

2. _____ that have made it

possible for them to live virtually

anywhere there is land. Insects have a

tough, jointed 3. _____ that

houses the organ systems. It is equipped

with 4. _____ organs that can detect

light, 5. _____ , temperature, and odour. The insect's body

is divided into 6. _____ segments: head, 7. _____ ,

and abdomen. They have three pairs of 8. _____ , muscles,

and body systems that take care of respiration, 9. _____ ,

reproduction, and digestion.

10.

11.

12.

D. Answer the questions with the given words.

thorax	arthropod	dragonfly	insects
exoskeleton	legs	sense organs	three

1. Which are the most diverse animals on the planet?

   _____

2. What do insects have so that they can detect light, sound, temperature, and odour?

   _____

3. What insect can fly up to speeds of 55 km/h?

   _____

4. Insects have three pairs of these. What are they?

   _____

5. What houses the many organs of an insect?

   _____

6. How many segments is an insect's body divided into?

   _____

7. Which section of an insect bears the legs and wings?

   _____

8. To what phylum do insects belong?

   _____

Science Corner . . . .

Did you know the cockroach is a special creature that can "live" for about a week with its head cut off?

2

Natural Sponges vs. Synthetic Sponges

Did you know that the natural sponge we use in the bath is actually a living sea animal? Sponges live on rocks deep in the ocean. Their bodies are filled with tiny holes, so water can flow through them. These give the sponges the ability of holding water and filtering dirt.

Ask your parents to buy you one or two natural sponges and a synthetic one. Make a chart to record their physical characteristics and find the amount of water each sponge can hold before dripping.

Before finding the amount of water each sponge can hold, make sure they are about the same size.

	Natural Sponge		Synthetic Sponge
	A	**B**	
Colour			
Softness			
Amount of water held (mL)			

Checklist

Are you able to…

- [ ] name some invertebrates?
- [ ] match invertebrates with the correct descriptions?
- [ ] describe and identify insects?
- [ ] answer questions related to insects?

Vertebrates (1)

backbone

3

Jason, can you see its big backbone? We are vertebrates; dinosaurs are vertebrates too.

In this unit, students will:

- learn about the classification system.
- identify the five classes of vertebrates.
- recognize the importance of skin to animals and match skin coverings with the correct animals.
- write the name of a vertebrate in each class, tell where it lives, and name the parts of the body that help it move about.

3

A. Read what Doctor Smith says. Answer the questions.

Carolus Linnaeus (1707 – 1778), a Swedish naturalist, developed the classification system that we use today. There are seven levels of classification. They are kingdom, phylum, class, order, family, genus, and species. Organisms in different kingdoms are very different from one another, while members of the same species are very similar.

Scientists have put organisms into groups based on their body structures. Animals with backbones are called vertebrates. They have an internal skeleton made of bones and both left and right parts of the body are the same. There are five classes of vertebrates.

1. Who developed the classification system?

     _____

2. How many levels of classification are there? What are they?

     _____

     _____

3. How did scientists put organisms into groups?

     _____

4. Do vertebrates have a symmetrical body structure? Explain.

     _____

     _____

B. **Read the characteristics that are used to group the vertebrates. Match them with the correct classes. Write the names. Then circle the correct animals.**

— Classes —

Amphibian   **Bird**   **Fish**   **Mammal**   **Reptile**

1.
Fish

- wet scales and mucus
- cold-blooded
- lay eggs

e.g. (shark) / owl

2.
Amphibian

- soft, moist, naked skin
- cold-blooded
- eggs laid by most

e.g. cow / (bullfrog)

3.
Bird

- feathers
- warm-blooded
- lay eggs

e.g. rattlesnake / (ostrich)

4.
Reptile

- overlapping dry scales
- cold-blooded
- eggs laid by most

e.g. cod / (crocodile)

5.

Mammal

- live birth; young nursed by mother
- warm-blooded
- hair or fur

e.g. (human being) / salamander

3

C. **Fill in the blanks with the given words. Then draw lines to match the body coverings with the correct animals.**

camouflage	skin	organs	barrier

1._____ is a very important

organ. It acts like a 2._____ ,

protecting the animal's inner

3._____ from the environment. It

can also 4._____ the animal, helping

it survive among predators and prey.

5.

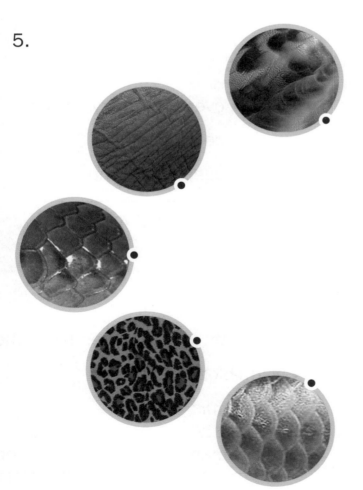

- elephant

- snake

- duck

- cheetah

- salmon

D. Write the name of a vertebrate that normally spends a good portion of its life living in that "space". Name the parts of the body that help it move about.

Class \ Space	On Land	In Water	In Air
Amphibian			
Bird			eagle (wings)
Fish		salmon (fins and tails)	
Mammal			
Reptile			

3

Guessing Game

You can play this game with your friends to see who is an animal expert.

Steps:

1. Have 20 cards ready and write the name of a vertebrate on each card.

2. Let your friends ask five questions about each animal.

3. The one who has the most correct guesses is the winner.

You may ask the following questions to know more about the animal on the card.

- What is the class of the animal?
- What is the colour of the body covering of the animal?
- Where does the animal live?
- What special adaptations has the animal made to survive?
- Does the animal have unique parts?

Are you able to…

- [ ] describe the classification system?
- [ ] identify the five classes of vertebrates?
- [ ] explain the importance of skin to animals and match skin coverings with the correct animals?
- [ ] write the name of a vertebrate in each class, tell where it lives, and name the parts of the body that help it move about?

Vertebrates (2)

In this unit, students will:

- identify the feeding actions of different vertebrates.
- identify the food of different vertebrates.
- identify the reproductive nature of different vertebrates.
- find out the relationship between the number of offspring produced and whether or not the parent raises the young.

4

A. **Fill in the blanks to complete what Joe says. Then match the vertebrates with their feeding actions. Write the letters.**

Vertebrates, as are living things, must "fit" the environment in which they live. They have special 1._____ that help them survive in their niche. All vertebrates must 2._____ in order to survive. All 3._____ and plants have their own special ways to get food.

eat
adaptations
animals

4.

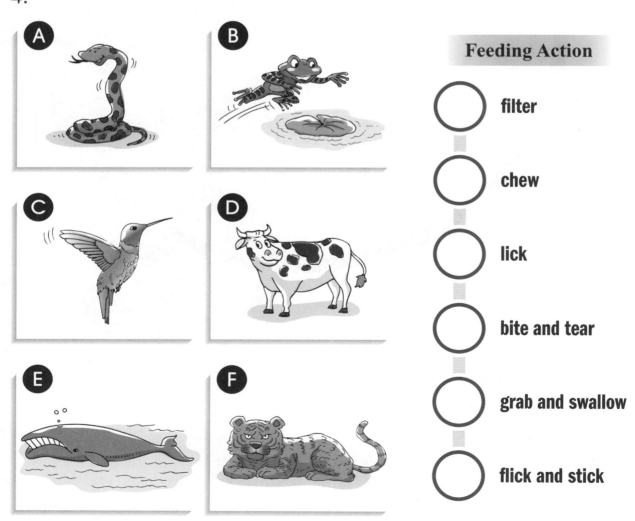

	Feeding Action
◯	filter
◯	chew
◯	lick
◯	bite and tear
◯	grab and swallow
◯	flick and stick

B. Look at the animals on the previous page again. Match them with the food. Write the letters. Then write another animal that uses the same feeding action to eat the food.

1.

◯ ; _____

2.

◯ ; _____

3.

◯ ; _____

4.

◯ ; _____

5.

◯ ; _____

6.

◯ ; _____

4

C. **Fill in the blanks with the given words to complete the paragraphs. Then give two more examples for each kind of vertebrates.**

life   offspring   reproduce   one

All living things must 1._____ . Without reproduction, there would be no more 2._____ on Earth.

Living things have many different ways of reproducing. Some vertebrates have many 3._____ at one time while others reproduce only 4._____ or a few at a time.

5.

Vertebrates that have

one or a few offspring at a time	many offspring at a time
panda	fish
human being	pig
_____	_____
_____	_____

D. Identify each of the creatures described below. Then state whether or not you think the parents would stay around to raise the offspring. Answer the question.

Sea turtle **Wood frog** **Great blue heron** **African elephant**

1. A typical female will give birth every four to six years. The newborn weighs 100 kg and stands about a metre in height.

_____

2. Some lay up to 800 eggs in a jelly mass...hatch in 15 to 20 days.

_____

3. A female will go up on the beach and lay up to 150 eggs in the sand. When they hatch, it's a wild scramble to the ocean. Watch out for the gulls.

_____

4. Three to seven eggs are laid in the spring.

_____

5.

What is the relationship between the number of offspring produced and whether or not the parent raises the young?

_____

_____

4

Animals' Offspring

Do some research on the reproduction of the animals listed below and complete the chart with your favourite animals. Then you may ask your friends to see whether or not they know about the reproduction of these animals.

Vertebrate	Number of offspring at a time
giraffe	*one*
brown bear	
rabbit	
parrot	
salmon	

How many offspring does it have at a time?

one

Find out more about vertebrates on pages 114 and 115.

Are you able to...

☐ identify the feeding actions of different vertebrates?

☐ identify the food of different vertebrates?

☐ identify the reproductive nature of different vertebrates?

☐ tell the relationship between the number of offspring produced and whether or not the parent raises the young?

Properties of Air (1)

38.5 kg

39 kg

Can you see that he weighs a bit more with all those inflated balloons? It's because air has weight.

In this unit, students will:

- find the evidence of air.
- recognize that air has weight.
- recognize that air expands when heated.

5

A. **There is evidence of air in this picture. Can you find nine things that indicate air is there? List them in the chart.**

Evidence of Air

bubble filled with air | balloon filled with air | candle flame blown out

chimney smoke blown sideways | fan induced moving air | wind blowing hat off

kite in air | pinwheel moving | basketball filled with air.

B. **Unscramble the letters to complete what Sue says. Then draw a balloon to make each set correct and circle the correct word.**

Anything with mass is pulled towards the Earth by the force of gravity. Your weight depends on your mass and the gravity pulling you down. Since 1. _air_ (ria) has mass, gravity is also pulling it down, so it must also have 2. _weight_ (wigeth).

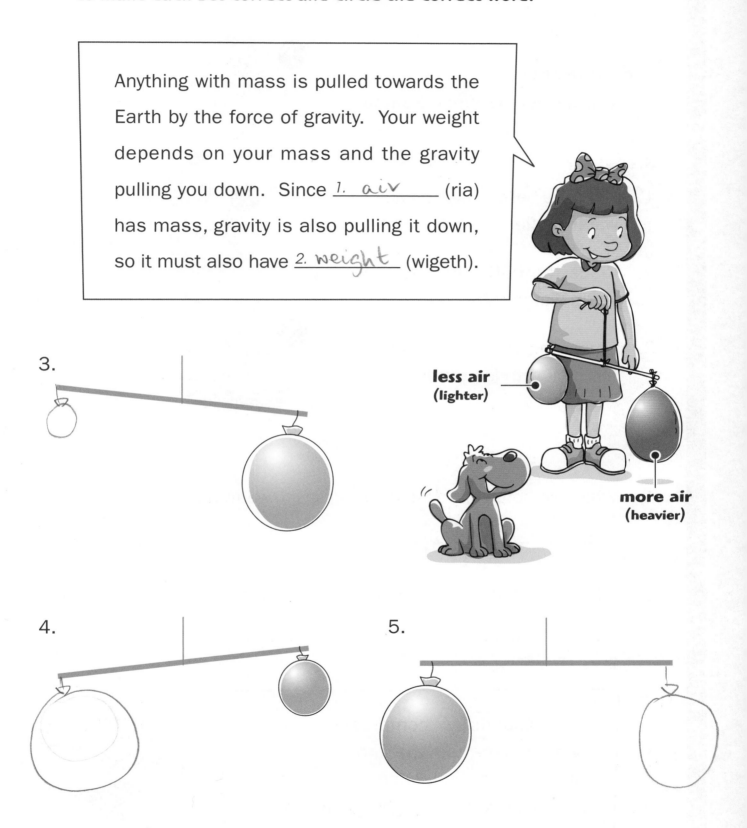

less air
(lighter)

more air
(heavier)

3.

4.

5.

6. The more air a balloon contains, the (heavier) / lighter the balloon is.

5

C. **Look at the experiment. Answer the questions and circle the correct words to complete what Mary says.**

Experiment:

How Air Reacts When Heated

Steps:

1. Stretch a balloon over an open, empty water bottle.

2. Place the bottle in a sink of very warm water.

3. Empty the warm water and fill the sink with ice water.

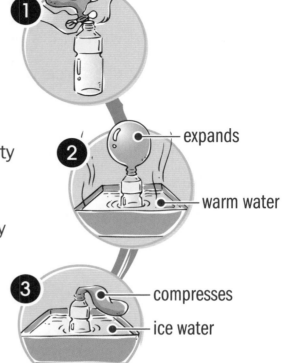

1

2 ── expands

── warm water

3 ── compresses

── ice water

1. When the bottle is placed in the sink with warm water, what happens?

    The warm water heats the air inside the bottle and the air expands to fill the balloon.

2. When the bottle is placed in the sink with ice water, what happens?

    The air inside the balloon cools and compresses. The balloon is deflated.

3.

> Air (expands) / compresses when heated because the molecules are further apart. This also has the effect of making warm air (lighter) / heavier .

D. Put the steps of the experiment in the correct order. Then fill in the blanks to complete what Marco says.

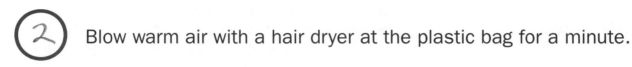

— Experiment: ————————————

Air Expands When Heated

Steps:

② Blow warm air with a hair dryer at the plastic bag for a minute.

① Blow up a plastic bag and twist it closed.

③ Observe the plastic bag.

The plastic bag _expands_ as the air inside expands when _heated_ .

E. Choose the correct words to complete the sentences.

1. Warm air meets cooler air. The warm air expands and _rises_ .
   rises / falls

2. A mobile hung from a ceiling is gently moving. The heat radiator below it is _on_ .
   on / off

3. A bird gliding in the sky is riding on the rising _warm_ air.
   warm / cool

4. The temperature in a house is normally cooler on the _bottom_ floor.
   bottom / top

5

Prove Air Has Weight

Materials:

- a 30-cm ruler
- newspaper

Air is pulled down by gravity just like all other matter. The difference in weight between an inflated balloon and a deflated balloon is very small. Consider the layer upon layer of air that press on the newspaper in this experiment. Will it have enough weight to keep the ruler from flying off the table?

Steps:

1. Put a ruler on a table so it is slightly hanging over the edge.

2. Lay a couple of open sheets of newspaper on the table, covering the part of the ruler that is on the table.

3. With a quick movement, hit the ruler with the side of your hand.

4. The paper itself does not have enough weight to prevent the ruler from falling. Do you know what provides the weight?

   _____

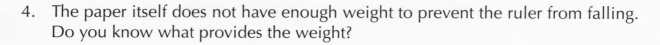

Checklist

Are you able to...

- [ ] find the evidence of air?
- [ ] show that air has weight?
- [ ] show that air expands when heated?

A. **Complete the crossword puzzle.**

Air has _____ .

animals with backbones

V E R T E B R A T E S

W E I G H T

R E P T I L E S

Insects have 3 pairs of _____ .

L E G S

M A M M A L S

M O L L U S K S

Insects have a tough, jointed _____ that houses the organ system.

E X O S K E L E T O N

S K I N

exoskeleton   legs   mammals   mollusks
reptiles   skin   vertebrates   weight

B. **Check the correct answers for each question.**

1. Vertebrates:

2. Invertebrates:

3. Characteristics of insects:

A   Their bodies are divided into three segments.

B   They have four pairs of legs.

C   They have scales and lungs.

D   They are equipped with sense organs that can detect light, sound, temperature, and odour.

4. Characteristics of reptiles:

(A) ✓ overlapping dry scales   (B) warm-blooded

(C) hair   (D) ✓ eggs laid by most

5. Properties of air:

(A) It expands when cooled.

(B) ✓ It expands when heated.

(C) ✓ Air has weight.

(D) Air is weightless.

6. The animals that have the same feeding action as the animal on the right:

(A) ✓

(B)

(C) ✓

(D)

7. Vertebrates that have one or a few offspring at a time:

(A) salmon   (B) ✓ koala

(C) ✓ horse   (D) turtle

C.   Match the characteristics of some major groups of invertebrates with the members. Write the letters.

Characteristics

A   segmented body covered by a hard exoskeleton with jointed legs

B   lives on its own or inside other animals, flat bodied, some members can regenerate body parts

C   soft body with a one- or two-part shell

D   spiny skinned, some with 5 rays or "arms" radiating from the middle of their bodies

E   soft, segmented body; some have bristles to aid in movement

Invertebrates

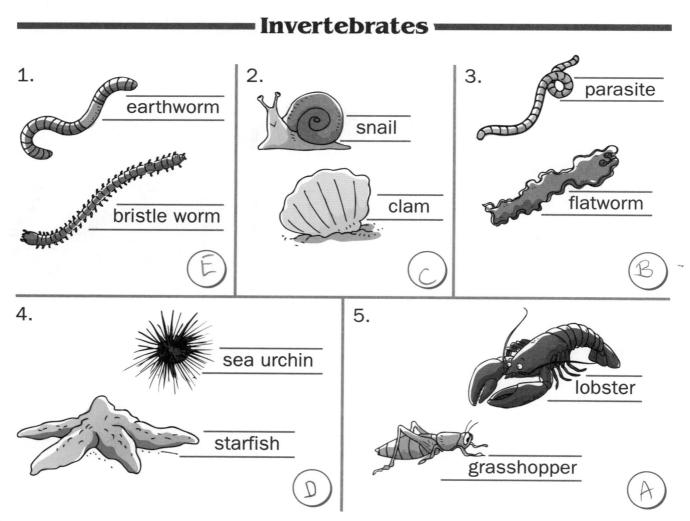

1.   earthworm
      bristle worm
      E

2.   snail
      clam
      C

3.   parasite
      flatworm
      B

4.   sea urchin
      starfish
      D

5.   lobster
      grasshopper
      A

D. **Write the names of the groups of the vertebrates. Then draw a picture of an animal that belongs to the group.**

Vertebrates

1.
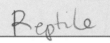
Reptile

- overlapping dry scales
- eggs laid by most
- cold-blooded

Example:

2.
Bird

- warm-blooded
- feathers
- lay eggs

Example:

3.

Fish

- wet scales and mucus
- cold-blooded
- lay eggs

Example:

4.
Amphibian

- soft, moist, naked skin
- cold-blooded
- eggs laid by most

Example:

5.

Mammal

- live birth; young nursed by mother
- warm-blooded
- hair or fur

Example:

E. Write an explanation for each experiment.

Experiment 1

Steps:

1. Have a glass of hot water ready.

2. Put a deformed table tennis ball in the glass.

3. The deformed table tennis ball recovers.

Why does this happen?

_____

_____

Experiment 2

Steps:

1. Inflate two balloons to about the same size and tie them each with a string.

2. Put a tape on one of the balloons.

3. Tie them each at the end of a rod to make a scale.

4. Poke a little hole on the tape with a pin.

5. One end of the scale weighs down.

Why does this happen?

_____

_____

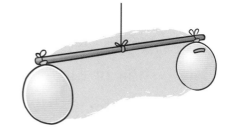

Properties of Air (2)

6

Warm air is trapped.

Thanks, Katie.

Grandma, I've knitted a woollen scarf for you. It's a good insulator because it traps warm air inside. I'm sure it'll keep you warm in winter.

In this unit, students will:

- recognize that air occupies space.
- recognize that air resists things moving through it.
- learn the compressibility and insulating quality of air.
- match the properties of air with air facts.

6

A. **Look at the experiment. Unscramble the letters to complete what Matt says. Then answer the question.**

Experiment: Air occupies space.

Steps:

1. Tuck a crumpled tissue tightly into the bottom of a glass.

2. Hold the glass upside down over a sink full of water and, without tilting the glass sideways, force it down into the water until it is fully immersed.

3. Pull the glass out of the water the same way.

The tissue stays _____dry_____ because
rdy

water can't enter the glass. It is already

full of _____air_____ . This experiment
ria

proves that air occupies _____space_____ .
esapc

What will happen if the glass is tilted sideways in step 2?

The air will leave the glass and water will enter to take its space. The tissue will be wet.

B. **Read what Timothy says. Try to do the experiment. Then check the correct answers.**

— *Experiment:* —

Air resists things moving through it.

Get 2 pieces of paper, identical in weight and size. Crumple one of them. Now, at the same time and from the same height, drop them. You can see that they don't hit the ground at the same time.

1. Which one hits the ground first? Why?

   (A) The paper is heavier after it is crumbled, so it falls to the ground before the intact paper.

   (B) ✓ The crumpled paper has less area for air to resist, and falls to the ground before the intact paper.

   (C) The crumpled paper has less area for air to resist, and falls to the ground after the intact paper.

2. Which events show that air resists things moving through it?

   (A) ✓ Leaves fall slowly to the ground.

   (B) A book is put on a blown-up balloon.

   (C) ✓ A parachutist jumps from a plane with a parachute.

   (D) A plastic bag filled with air is poked.

6

C. Fill in the blanks with the given words. Then write the letters in the correct boxes.

Two qualities of air enable us to use it as a useful tool. Air can be _1. compressed_ , and air can act as an _2. insulator_ .

Air is compressed when more than the regular amount of air has been pushed into a container. More air in the same space exerts _3. more_ pressure.

Air acts as an insulator when it helps _4. conserve_ heat. The fur of my dog works in this way by trapping air to keep itself warm.

conserve
more
compressed
insulator

5.

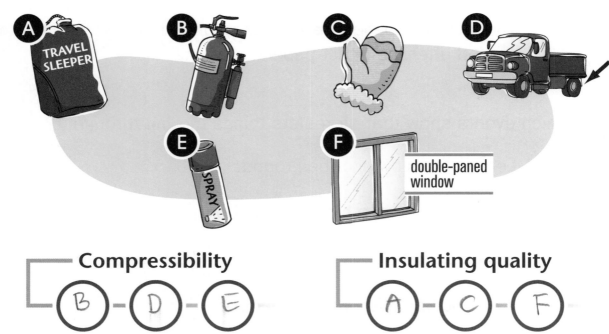

Compressibility
B – D – E

Insulating quality
A – C – F

D. Match each fact with the property of air. Write the letter.

Properties of Air

A Air has weight.

B Air takes up space.

C Air presses on things.

D Air can be compressed.

E Air resists things moving through it.

F Air expands when heated.

G Air has insulating quality.

Air Facts

1. A flat car tire is lighter than when it was full of air.
 A

2. A flat piece of paper falls slower to the ground than a crumpled piece of paper.
 E

3. Air molecules move around and spread out when heated.
 F

4. Air expands to fill a container, but we may still put more air in it.
 D

5. A feather down coat traps air within it. It keeps the warmth in and the cold out.
 G

6. An "empty" water bottle immersed in water upside down will not fill with water because it is already full of air.
 B

7. A card placed over the rim of a cup of water will hold the water in place while the cup is upside down. The only thing holding the card in place is the air underneath the card.
 C

6

Air Presses on Things!

Materials:

- a glass with a smooth rim
- a glossy card
- water

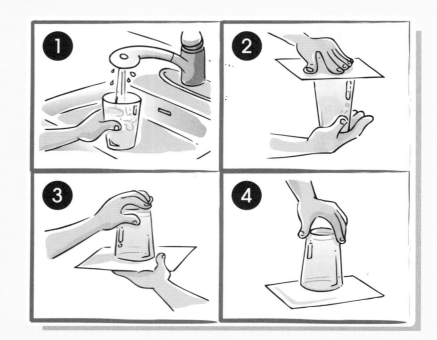

Steps:

1. Fill the glass to the rim with water.

2. Place the glossy side of the card down on the rim of the glass.

3. Keep the palm of your hand on the card and turn the glass upside down.

4. Take your hand away from the card.

> The card remains attached to the rim of the glass. The water does not fall out. Do you know why?

Answer:

The air pressure exerted on the card from underneath is greater than the weight of the water in the glass. This is why the card can hold the water in the glass.

Checklist

Are you able to...

- [ ] show that air occupies space?
- [ ] show that air resists things moving through it?
- [ ] identify the compressibility and insulating quality of air?
- [ ] match the properties of air with air facts?

Characteristics of Flight (1)

7

lift

faster air; lower pressure

slower air; higher pressure

How can she fly with those "wings"?

In this unit, students will:

- learn about Bernoulli's Principle.
- learn what airfoil is and identify structures that are examples of airfoil.
- describe the sources of propulsion for flying devices.

7

A. Complete the paragraphs with the given words. Then complete the diagram.

> Bernoulli   lower   lift   higher

For something heavier than air to fly is to work against gravity. This can be done by providing 1. _lift_ , using what we call 2. _Bernoulli_ 's Principle.

Bernoulli's Principle states that the faster the air moves, the 3. _lower_ the pressure it exerts. That means when the air above an object moves faster than the air below it, the air pressure pushing up on the bottom of the object is 4. _higher_ than the pressure pushing down, so the object goes up.

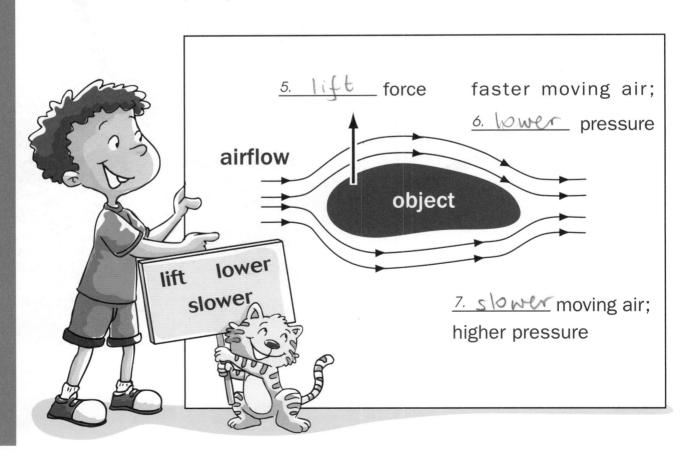

5. _lift_ force   faster moving air;
6. _lower_ pressure

airflow

object

lift   lower   slower

7. _slower_ moving air;
higher pressure

B. **What will happen in these instances of unbalanced air pressure? Draw arrows to show the movements of the objects caused by unbalanced air pressure and complete the explanations.**

1.

Explanation:

The air underneath the paper moves faster which causes a _decrease_ (**edsarcee**) in pressure. The higher pressure on top of the paper pushes the paper _down_ (**wdon**) toward the table.

2.

Explanation:

The airflow across the top surface of the paper exerts a pressure that is _less_ (**elss**) than the air pressure underneath. The air pressure underneath the paper is _higher_ (**ihghre**), which makes the paper _rise_ (**srie**).

7

C. **Fill in the blanks to complete the paragraph. Then check the pictures that are examples of airfoil providing lift.**

airfoil	lift	below	faster

Bernoulli's Principle helps explain how an airplane or a bird can gain

1. *lift* , the force that acts against gravity. The shape of a wing is

called an 2. *airfoil* , and is the cause of the unbalanced air pressure

above and 3. *below* the wing. The

air must move farther and 4. *faster*

over the top of the wing.

5.

Examples of Airfoil

D. **Read what Brian says. Match the flying machine or animal with its source of propulsion.**

Thrust is the force that propels something through the air.

Thrust

A propeller

B engine

C moving air

D wings

E rocket

F human muscle energy

1.

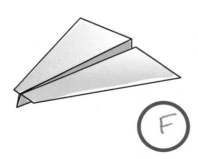

E

2.

D

3.

C

4.

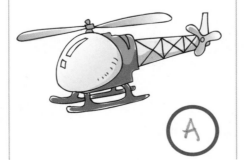

F

5.

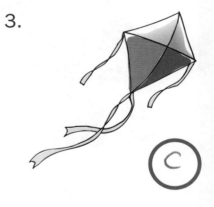

A

6.

B

7

A Paper Airplane

Material:

- a sheet of 22 cm x 28 cm paper

Steps:

(Fold along the dotted lines shown in the directions of the arrows.)

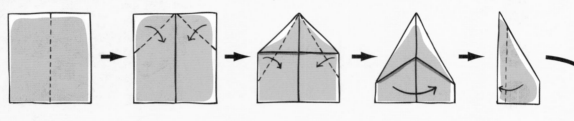

Make 2 cuts on either side of the centre fold. Then fold the flaps up.

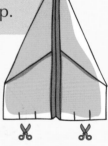

A paper airplane uses lift to remain in flight until it uses up the force of the thrust from your hand. Ask your friends to make paper airplanes and play with them to see whose paper airplane flies the best.

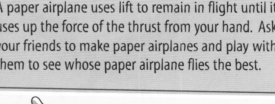

Checklist

Are you able to...

- [ ] explain Bernoulli's Principle?
- [ ] explain what airfoil is and identify structures that are examples of airfoil?
- [ ] describe the sources of propulsion for flying devices?

Characteristics of Flight (2)

8

I have a strong thrust.

Look! When the balloon is let go, the air inside bursts out of the mouth of the balloon. This creates a backward thrust which makes the balloon "fly".

In this unit, students will:

- learn about the force of drag and show it in different examples.
- understand the meaning of streamline and identify objects that have a streamlined form.
- learn the relationships among the forces that make an airplane fly.
- use different words to describe the characteristics of flight.

8

A. **Fill in the blanks to complete what Ricky says. Then draw an arrow to show the drag in each picture.**

balanced   drag   increased

The force opposing thrust is _1. drag_ . Drag is what must be overcome for something to move forward through air. Drag must be _2. increased_, though, to slow down or stop. An airplane flying at a steady speed has a _3. balanced_ force of thrust and drag.

4.

5.

6.

B.   Fill in the missing letters. Then check the object or animal in each group that has a streamlined form.

1.

> When something is built to reduce drag, we say it is s t r eamli n e d . Streamlining helps reduce d r a g on the ground and in the water, as well as in the a i r .

2.   (A)   (B) ✓

3.   (A)   (B) ✓   (C)

4.   (A)   (B)   (C) ✓

8

C. **Read the paragraph. Label the diagram with the words in bold. Then answer the questions.**

*Something flying at a steady speed has balanced forces of **thrust** and **drag**. If it is flying at a steady altitude, it has balanced forces of **gravity** and **lift**. Sometimes the forces are not balanced. For example, in order to go faster, the force of thrust must be increased.*

1.

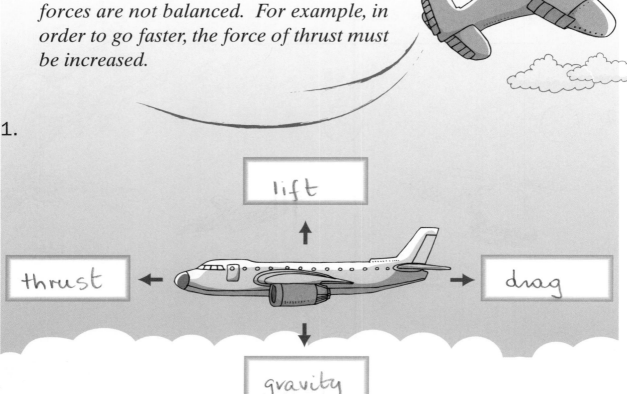

lift

thrust

drag

gravity

2. Which two forces have to be increased in order for the airplane to ↑ascend?

   <u>thrust and lift</u>

3. Which two forces are balanced when the airplane is flying at a steady altitude?

   <u>lift and gravity</u>

D. Write the given words on the lines to match the descriptions.

> drag   Bernoulli   dragonfly
> streamlined   thrust   lift

1. the force that slows down a moving body   _drag_

2. a term describing a shape that offers minimum resistance to fluid flow   _streamlined_

3. family name of a famous Swiss mathematician and scientist   _Bernoulli_

4. a forward-directed force   _thrust_

5. the force acting on an airfoil, opposing the force of gravity   _lift_

6.

a member of the group of the oldest known fliers in nature that is able to do a somersault and land upside down on a ceiling

dragonfly

8

A Jet-Propelled Balloon

Materials:

- a string
- tape
- a drinking straw
- a balloon

Steps:

1. Thread the string through the straw and tie the ends tightly at two points of equal height in a room.

2. Inflate the balloon and keep it closed with fingers.

3. Tape the balloon underneath the straw and pull the balloon to one end of the string.

4. Let go of the balloon.

What happens?

_____

Do you know why?

_____

_____

Checklist

Are you able to...

☐ explain the force of drag and show it in different examples?

☐ explain the meaning of streamline and identify objects that have a streamlined form?

☐ describe the relationships among the forces that make an airplane fly?

☐ use different words to describe the characteristics of flight?

Static and Current Electricity (1)

static electricity — | — current electricity

In this unit, students will:

- identify electrical devices or machines in daily life.
- describe and identify static electricity and current electricity.
- learn about conductors and insulators and identify objects that are conductors and insulators.
- learn how a closed circuit is built and tell whether the circuits are closed or not.

9

A. **Where is electricity in our daily lives? List the electrical devices and machines you see in each picture. Then give one more example that could go in the picture.**

1. **Office**

lamp	computer	telephone	
printer	clock	photocopier	calculator

2. **Home**

refrigerator	oven	microwave	
range hood	stove	coffee maker	toaster

B. **Fill in the blanks to complete the paragraph. Then tell whether each picture shows static electricity or current electricity.**

current   heat   rubbed   static

1. _Static_ electricity is what you feel when you touch a doorknob after shuffling across the carpet, or when a sock sticks to your sweater after coming out of the dryer. Things can become electrically charged when they are 2. _rubbed_ .

3. _Current_ electricity is very useful to us. It can be transformed into light, 4. _heat_ , or motion energy.

5.

static electricity

6.

current electricity

7.

static electricity

8.

current electricity

9

C. **Fill in the blanks to complete what Judy the Robot says. Then put the things in the correct boxes and write the answers.**

1.

a conductor

an insulator

A _conductor_ is a substance that allows electric current to flow through it. We use these materials to build circuits.

An _insulator_ is a substance that does not allow electric current to flow through it.

2.

Conductor

juice
towel
fork

Insulator

eraser
ball
book

3. Using the information above, write "conductor" or "insulator" to describe the materials below.

a. rubber _insulator_

b. water _conductor_

c. wood _insulator_

d. metal _conductor_

D. **Look at each circuit. Circle the problem area or write "closed circuit" if it is one.**

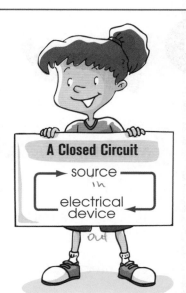

For an electric current to flow, it must have a continuous route to travel. It must go from the source, through the electrical device, and back to the source. That is called a closed circuit.

A Closed Circuit

source → in → electrical device → out

1.

_____ circuit

2.

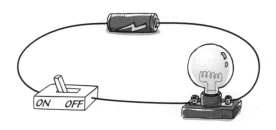

closed circuit

3.

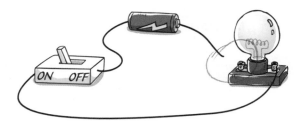

closed circuit

4.

_____

5.

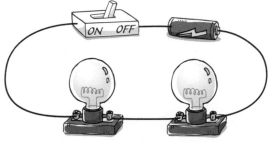

battery missing

_____

6.

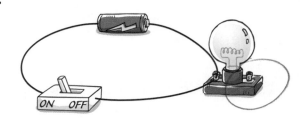

closed circuit

9

"Static" Balloons

Materials:

- 2 balloons

- a piece of nylon material

- a piece of wool material

Inflate the balloons. Rub them with different materials and then bring them close together to see what happens. Record your observations.

Experiment 1: Rub the balloons with the nylon material.

Observation: _____

Experiment 2: Rub the balloons with the wool material.

Observation: _____

Experiment 3: Rub one of the balloons with the nylon material and the other with the wool material.

Observation: _____

Can you explain why the balloons attract or repel each other?

_____

_____

Checklist

Are you able to...

☐ identify electrical devices or machines in daily life?

☐ describe and identify static electricity and current electricity?

☐ explain what conductors and insulators are and identify objects that are conductors and insulators?

☐ tell the meaning of a closed circuit and identify closed circuits?

Static and Current Electricity (2)

Mom, I know that these bulbs are connected in a parallel circuit. If one of them burns out, the others will still operate.

In this unit, students will:

- use symbols for different components to draw circuits.
- identify closed circuits.
- learn about series circuits and parallel circuits and identify them.
- solve problems about series circuits and parallel circuits.

10

A. Label the symbols with the given words.

To draw circuits, we use a symbol for each component. The different symbols make up the "language" of circuits.

bulb
cell
switch
wire

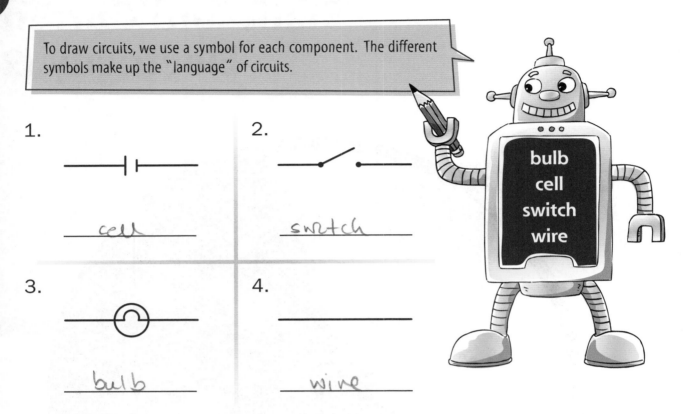

1.

cell

2.

switch

3.

bulb

4.

wire

B. Name the components in each circuit.

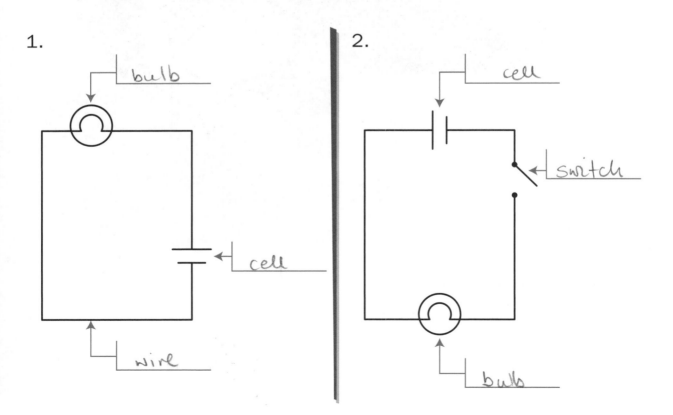

1.

bulb

cell

wire

2.

cell

switch

bulb

C. Look at the circuits. Circle the problem area if there is something preventing the flow of current. Write "CC" if it is a closed circuit.

1.

_____

2.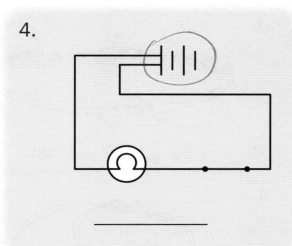

_____ CC _____

3.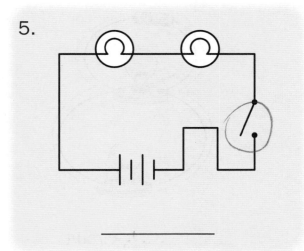

_____ CC _____

4.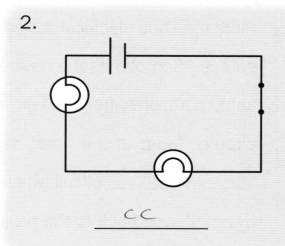

_____

5.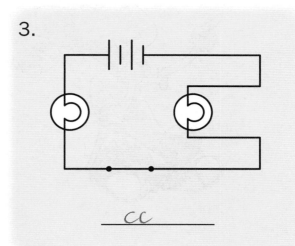

_____

6.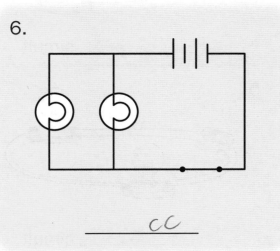

_____ CC _____

10

D. **Fill in the blanks and label the diagrams with the given words.**

More than one electrical device can share the same power source. Sometimes the devices are connected along the same path, one after another. This is a _1. Series_ circuit. Most of the time, devices are connected in a _2. parallel_ circuit, where they individually have their own path and back to the power source.

parallel

series

3.

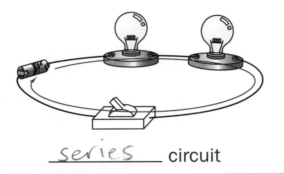

series circuit

4.

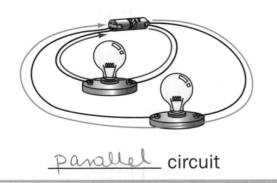

parallel circuit

6.

5.

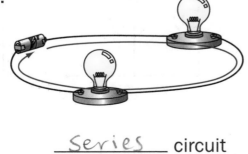

series circuit

parallel circuit

E. **Are the circuits parallel or in series? List them in the correct boxes. Then answer the questions.**

1.

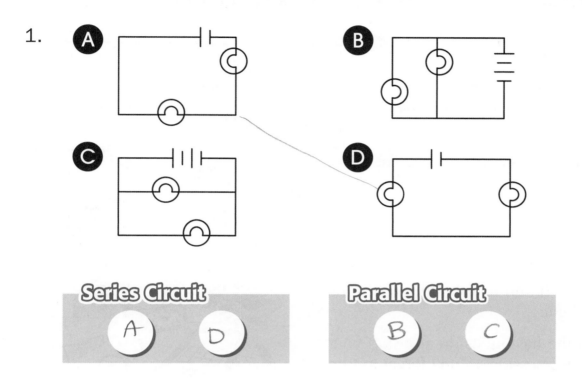

Series Circuit	Parallel Circuit
A D	B C

2.

What would happen to circuit A if one of the light bulbs burned out?

The pathway would be broken and the current of electricity would not flow. The other light bulb would not operate.

3.

What would happen to circuit B if one of the light bulbs burned out?

The pathway to the other light bulb would remain open to the flow of electricity. The other light bulb would operate.

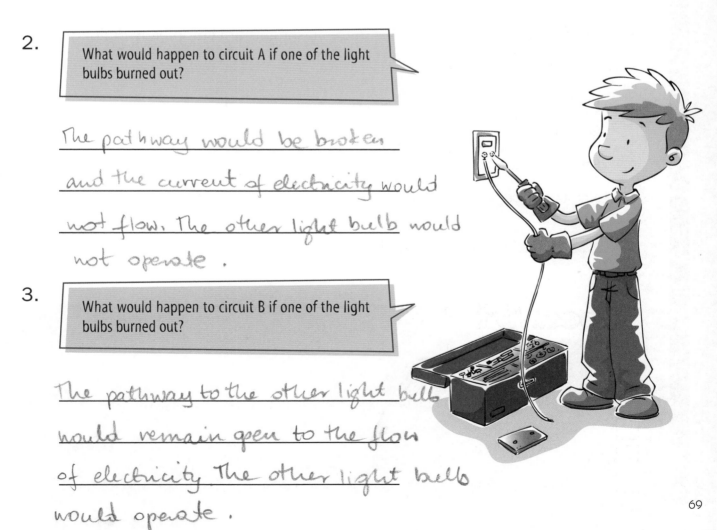

10

The Life of a Battery

Materials:

- 2 identical flashlights
  (the ones using two AA batteries
  to operate)

- 4 AA batteries from two different
  brands, two from each brand

- a clock

Let's study 2 hours every day and do this experiment at the same time to find out which brand of batteries lasts longer. Then compare the unit price and find the rate to see which one is the better buy!

Steps:

1. Put the brand new batteries into the
   flashlights.

2. Turn the flashlights on and start your
   studying session. Don't forget to turn
   off the flashlights after each session.

3. Repeat step 2 until the batteries in the flashlights are completely drained.

Record your observations.

Brand		
Starting Date		
Finishing Date		
Number of Days They Lasted		

_____ is the better buy.

Are you able to...

☐ use symbols for different components to draw circuits?

☐ identify closed circuits?

☐ explain what series circuits and parallel circuits are and identify them?

☐ solve problems about series circuits and parallel circuits?

A. Complete the crossword puzzle.

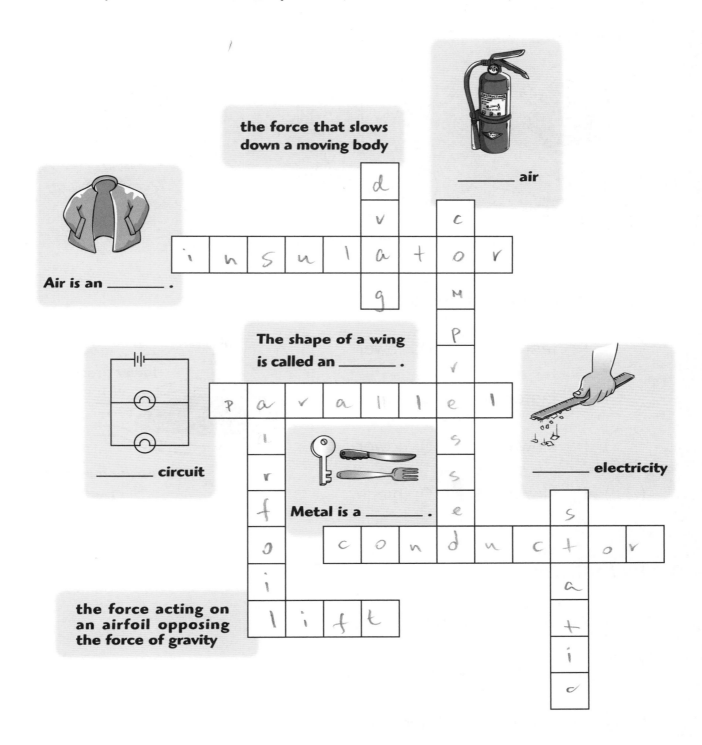

the force that slows down a moving body

_____ air

Air is an _____ .

The shape of a wing is called an _____ .

_____ circuit

_____ electricity

Metal is a _____ .

the force acting on an airfoil opposing the force of gravity

Crossword answers:

d
v
i n s u l a t o r
g

c
o
M
p
r
e
s
s
e

P a r a l l e l

p
a
r
f
o
i
l   i f t

c o n d u c t o r

s
t
a
t
i
c

airfoil   compressed   conductor   drag
insulator   lift   parallel   static

B. **Check the correct answers.**

1. Conductors:

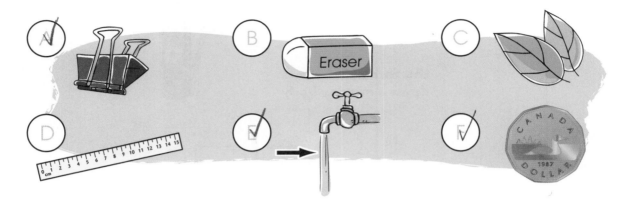

2. The missing terms in the diagram:

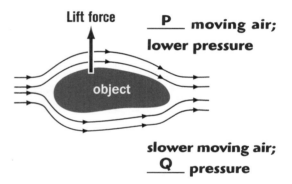

(A) P: faster   Q: lower

(B) P: faster   Q: higher

(C) P: slower   Q: lower

(D) P: slower   Q: higher

3. Properties of air:

(A) Air cannot be compressed.

(B)   Air resists things moving through it.

(C)   Air has insulating quality.

(D)   Air expands when heated.

(E) Air is weightless.

(F)   Air takes up space.

4. Examples of static electricity:

5. The closed circuits:

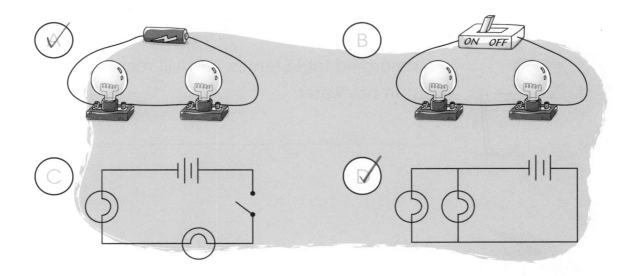

6. Ones that have a streamlined form:

C. Which property of air is shown in each event? Write the answer on the line.

Properties of Air

- Air occupies space.
- Air resists things flowing through it.
- Air expands when heated.
- Air has insulating quality.

1.

Leaves fall slowly to the ground.

Air resists things flowing through it

2.

A deformed table tennis ball will recover when it is put in hot water.

Air expands when heated

3.

A blown-up balloon does not flatten when a book is placed on it.

Air occupies space

4.

The hot water in the jar wrapped in woollen cloth cools slower than the hot water in the unwrapped jar.

Air has insulating quality.

D. **Look at the circuits. Use symbols to complete the matching diagrams. Then answer the questions.**

1.

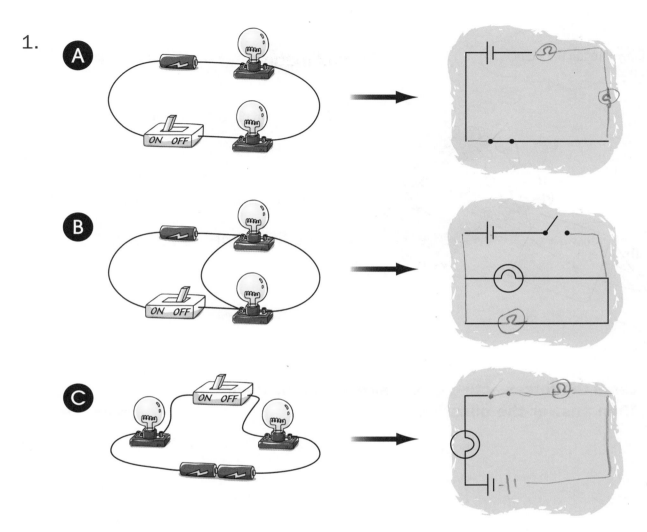

2.

Which circuits are in series?

_____ A , C _____

3.

If one of the bulbs in a series circuit burns out, what happens to the whole circuit?

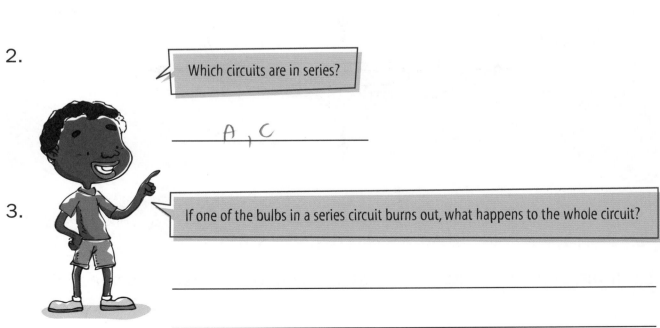

_____

_____

E. Draw arrows to show the movement of the paper caused by the unbalanced air pressure. Then complete the explanation.

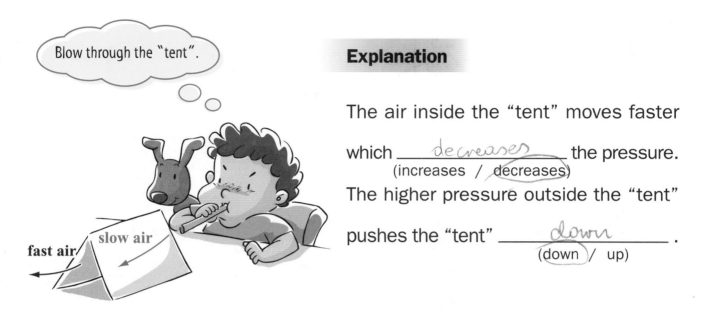

Blow through the "tent".

fast air / slow air

Explanation

The air inside the "tent" moves faster

which ___decreases___ the pressure.
(increases / ~~decreases~~)

The higher pressure outside the "tent"

pushes the "tent" ___down___ .
(~~down~~ / up)

F. Label the forces acting on the airplane in the diagram. Then answer the question.

lift
gravity
drag
thrust

1.

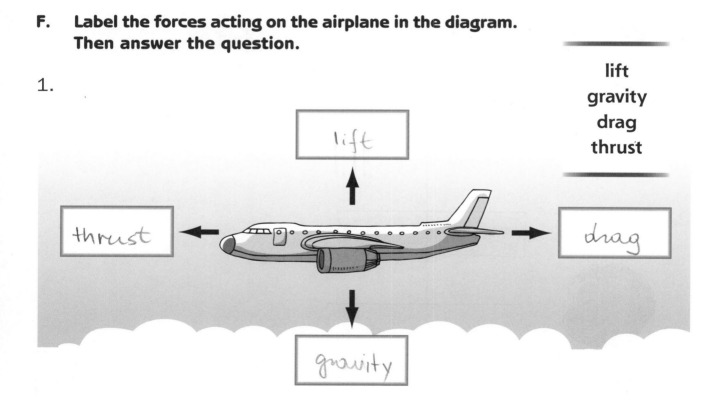

lift

thrust

drag

gravity

2. If the airplane wants to go faster, which force must be increased?

_____

More about Electricity

Sam, I think we don't need this because the show is about the life of people living 300 years ago when there was no electricity. So, what we need are candles.

In this unit, students will:

- learn about the discovery of electricity.
- compare modern activities that use electricity with similar activities before electricity was used.
- name the common sources of electric power and tell whether they are renewable or non-renewable.

11

A. **Read what Fred says and the paragraphs below. Then check the correct sentences.**

What led us to be using electricity the way we do today? Ancient peoples, it is believed, knew about current electricity. But that didn't lead them to use it. Luigi Galvani and Allessandro Volta were two people who experimented and learned a lot about electricity.

More than 200 years ago in Italy, scientist Luigi Galvani accidentally brought two different metals together during a dead frog dissection and caused the frog's leg to twitch. Galvani wondered if he had discovered an electrical force in the frog's body. He didn't. But what he did discover was a kind of electricity that was very different from static electricity and lightning.

Allessandro Volta invented the first battery around 1800. Galvani's discovery helped him in this invention, which used two different metals and salty water. Before the invention of battery, electric machines worked on static electricity, and only for very short periods.

(A) Volta did experiments on frogs.

(B) ✓ Galvani was using two different kinds of metals.

(C) ✓ These discoveries took place about 200 years ago.

(D) Electric machines once worked only with lightning.

(E) Volta's invention was independent of other discoveries.

(F) ✓ What Galvani discovered was different from static electricity and lightning.

B. **Draw lines to match the modern activities that use electricity with similar activities before electricity was used. Then write the answer.**

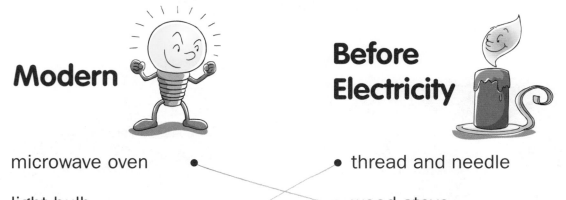

Electricity has only been in common use for the last hundred years or so. What was life like before electricity was used?

1.

Modern

Before Electricity

microwave oven ●   ● thread and needle

light bulb ●   ● wood stove

sewing machine ●   ● wringer washer and clothesline

washer and dryer ●   ● gas lamp

people watching TV ●   ● people talking, playing games

computer ●   ● manual typewriter, paper, and pen

2.

List three other things you use today that are powered by electricity. Then guess what had been used in their place in the time before electricity was in common use.

_____

_____

_____

_____

_____

11

C. Name the common sources of electric power. Read the descriptions and match them with the sources. Then tell whether they are "renewable" or "non-renewable".

solar panels   wind farm   oil rig
hydroelectric dam   coal power generator
nuclear power generator

1.

<u>hydroelectric dam</u>

2.

<u>solar panels</u>

3.

<u>wind farm</u>

4.

<u>oil rig</u>

5.

<u>coal power generator</u>

6.

<u>nuclear power generator</u>

7.

Heat energy and light energy from the sun is less polluting but expensive to collect.

solar panels ;

renewable

8. Millions of years ago, it was dead plants and animals; now we find the liquid between layers of rocks underground.

oil rig ; _non-renewable_

9. It is produced with the help of the mineral uranium; the waste this form of energy produces is long-lived and dangerous.

nuclear power generator _non-renewable_

10. It takes millions of years in the making; this underground solid is a serious pollutant when burned for energy.

coal power generator; _non-renewable_

11. It is not polluting, but the negative impact dams have on the physical environment and nature is large.

hydroelectric dam; _renewable_

12. Windmills transform moving air to electricity. They are less polluting, but they are not without problems.

wind farm ;

renewable

Find out more about electricity on pages 116 and 117.

Battery Care

Test yourself to see whether or not you know how to take care of and handle your batteries. Put a check mark in the battery if you do the following; otherwise, put a cross.

Keep battery contact surfaces clean by gently rubbing them with a cloth.

Replace batteries with the size and type specified by the manufacturer of the device.

Store batteries in a dry place at normal temperature.

Do not dispose of batteries in a fire.

Prevent crushing, puncturing, or excessive pressure on batteries.

Keep spare batteries in their original retail packaging.

Keep loose batteries covered with insulating tape to protect them from contact with metal objects.

If you checked all the batteries, you are really smart at handling batteries. You can do this activity with your friends and let them know how to be battery-smart, too.

Do not mix old and new batteries, or mix different types of batteries. This can cause leakage or rupture.

Checklist

Are you able to...

- tell about the discovery of electricity?
- compare modern activities that use electricity with similar activities before electricity was used?
- name the common sources of electric power and tell whether they are renewable or non-renewable?

Motion

12

oscillating motion

reciprocating motion

rotational motion

linear motion

In this unit, students will:

- identify and describe different kinds of motion.
- draw motion paths and name the motions.
- find ways to increase or reduce friction in different situations.

12

A. Look at the examples of different motions. Fill in the missing letters to complete the words. Then fill in the blanks with the given words.

linear	oscillating	circular path	one direction
reciprocating	rotational	straight line	back-and-forth

Motions:

1.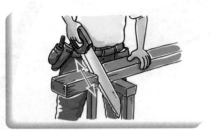

   r_e_ _c_ip_r_ _o_ _c_at_i_ _n_ _g_ motion
   - a back-and-forth movement in a
     straight line

2.

   _r_ot_a_ _t_i_o_ _n_al motion
   - a motion in a _circular path_

3.

   _l_ _i_ne_a_ _r_ motion
   - a motion in a straight line and in
     one direction

4.

   _o_sc_i_ _l_ _l_at_i_ _n_g motion
   - a motion _back-and-forth_ in a
     central point

B. How do these things move? Trace the dotted lines to show the motion paths. Then name the movements.

1.

reciprocating motion

2.

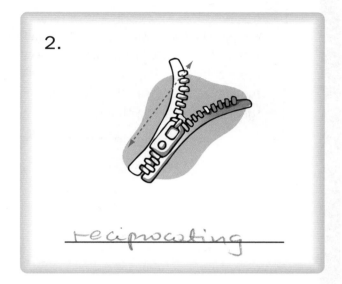

reciprocating

3.

rotational

4.

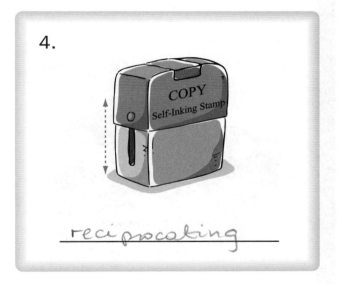

reciprocating

5.

oscillating

6.

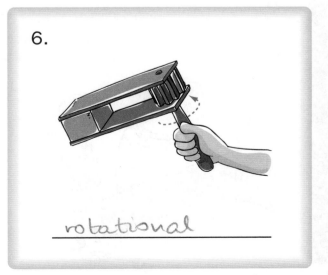

rotational

12

C. **Do the people need to increase or reduce friction? Write "increase" or "reduce" on the lines. Then check the correct methods.**

An object in motion will stay in motion until another force acts on it. The force that no moving object on Earth can avoid is friction. Friction is the force of two surfaces rubbing against each other. It is stronger with rough surfaces and weaker with smooth or wet surfaces.

I can run fast on rough surfaces with the help of friction.

1.

I can hear the metal grinding!

- _reduce_ friction

   (A) ✓ add oil to the engine

   (B) dry the engine

2.

How can I walk with higher stability on the balance beam?

- _increase_ friction

   (A) wear socks

   (B) ✓ walk barefoot

3.

How can I run faster?

- _increase_ friction

  (A) wear shoes without treads

  (B) ✓ wear shoes with treads

4.

I want to increase the speed of my car.

- _reduce_ friction

  (A) ✓ drive a streamlined racing car

  (B) drive a heavy racing car

5.

I want to slide down the slide at a higher speed.

- _reduce_ friction

  (A) ✓ add water from hose to the slide

  (B) dry the slide

12

Friction

Materials:

- a piece of sandpaper
- two identical small but heavy blocks
- two identical elastic bands
- tape
- some tacks

I think we need more effort to pull the block across the sandpaper. Am I correct?

Steps:

1. Pull the elastic bands at the same time and notice how much the elastic bands are stretched.

2. Compare the stretches and notice the effort needed to pull the blocks.

Observation

_____

Explanation

_____

_____

Are you able to...

- [ ] identify and describe different kinds of motion?
- [ ] draw motion paths and name the motions?
- [ ] find ways to increase or reduce friction in different situations?

Motion and Machines

13

Third-Class Lever

There are three classes of levers, each having the fulcrum, load, and effort in different positions.

Second-Class Lever

First-Class Lever

F: Fulcrum
L: Load
E: Effort

In this unit, students will:

- identify and name simple machines and identify machines that have rotational motion.
- learn the three classes of levers and find objects that belong to each class of lever.
- design a lever for a given situation.
- learn the meaning of a linkage system.

13

A. Identify the simple machines. Then answer the question.

lever	wedge	inclined plane
pulley	screw	wheel and axle

1.

A — screw

B — wheel and axle

C — wedge

D — inclined plane

E — lever

2.

pulley

3.

screw

4.

wedge

5.

Which machines above use rotational motion?

screw, pulley
wheel and axle

B. **Fill in the blanks to complete the definitions of the three classes of levers. Then cross out the one that does not belong to each class of lever.**

Classes of Levers:

First-Class Lever

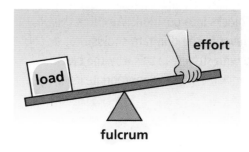

The fulcrum is in the centre, between the load and the _effort_ .

e.g.

Second-Class Lever

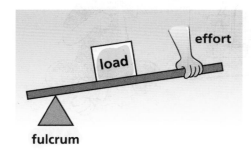

The fulcrum is at one end of the lever arm and the _effort_ is at the other end. The load is between them.

e.g.

Third-Class Lever

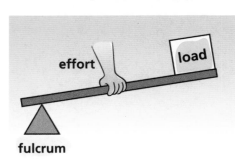

The _fulcrum_ is at one end and the load is at the other end. The effort is between them.

e.g.

13

C. **Read what Tony says. Help him design a lever to lift a huge pumpkin onto a wagon. Don't forget to show the load (pumpkin) and the effort force (effort) in your drawing.**

Egyptian pyramids were built from heavy and large blocks of limestones. It is believed that a mechanical crane of some form was used to lift the blocks into position. We think the Egyptians may have used levers to do the work. The lever in the diagram shows that a block is balanced by the weight of a wooden crate filled with stones. In this way, the block can be lifted by a person "pulling" the rope. Once the block reached the appropriate level, it would be "swung" into position using the lever.

Legend

lever arm	▭
fulcrum	△
load	⟶
effort	••▶

You may use the same technique shown in the diagram above.

D. Read what Boris says. Look at the linkage systems. Then trace the arrows to show the directions of movements and describe the diagrams.

● fixed fulcrum

○ moving fulcrum

A linkage system is two or more levers working together. They can change the direction of a motion or make two mechanisms work together.

1. a tool box

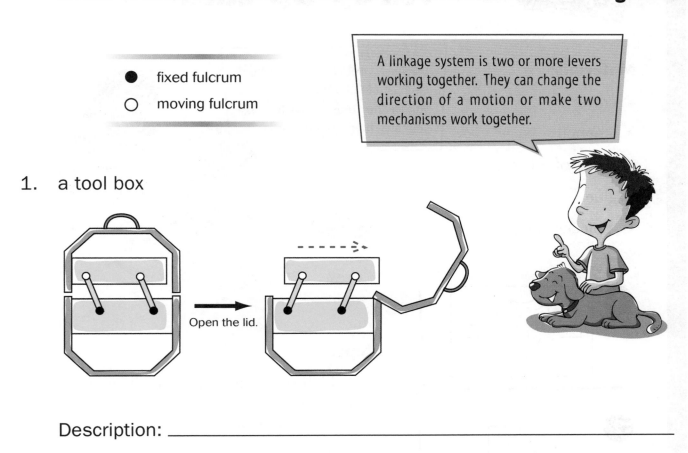

Open the lid.

Description: _____

2. a paper clown

Pull the yellow bar.

Description: _____

13

A Pop-Up Card

Materials:

- crayons
- a pencil
- a pair of scissors
- glue
- 2 pieces of paper

Did you know that a pop-up card is an example of a linkage system? Follow the steps below to make your own funny pop-up card.

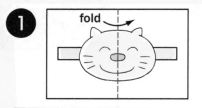

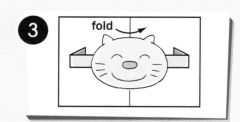

Steps:

1. Fold the paper in half. Open it and draw your favourite animal symmetrically with tabs on both sides. Colour the picture.

2. Cut out the picture and fold it.

3. Fold another piece of paper and then open it. Fold the ends of the tabs of the picture and glue the folded ends onto the paper. Make the fold line on the picture inside out.

4. Close the paper and open it. Done!

Checklist

Are you able to...

- [ ] identify and name simple machines and identify machines that have rotational motion?
- [ ] explain the differences and tell objects that belong to each of the three classes of levers?
- [ ] design a lever for a given situation?
- [ ] tell what a linkage system is?

Earth and Our Solar System

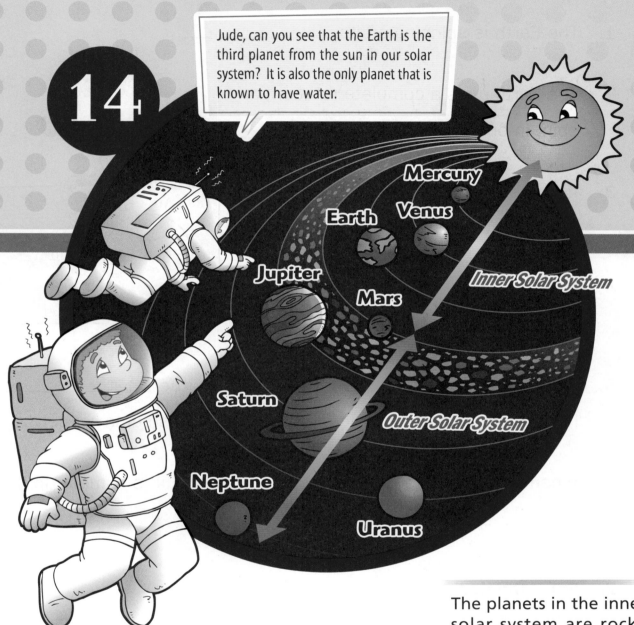

Jude, can you see that the Earth is the third planet from the sun in our solar system? It is also the only planet that is known to have water.

In this unit, students will:

- learn the relationship between the Earth and the sun.
- identify the phases of the moon.
- describe the physical characteristics of the planets in our solar system.
- use correct words to describe some objects in space.

The planets in the inner solar system are rocky planets.

The planets in the outer solar system are gaseous planets.

14

A. Look at the diagram. Fill in the blanks with the given words.

axis	day	northern	orbit	southern	year

1. The Earth is spinning on its ___axis___ .

2. The Earth does a complete rotation, or spin, in one ___day___ .

3. It takes one ___year___ for the Earth to travel around the sun.

The Earth

sunrays

4. The path of the Earth around the sun is called an ___orbit___ .

5. When the Earth is to the left of the sun, the ___northern___ hemisphere is getting more direct sunlight. It is summer there.

6. When the Earth is on the right side of the sun, it is summer in the ___southern___ hemisphere.

B. Solve the riddle.

What lights our night sky, yet emits no light?
What's always a sphere but seems different each night?
What spins round, yet shows only one side?
What causes, on Earth, the high and low tides?

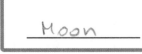

___Moon___

C. Fill in the blanks to complete what Peter says. Then name the different phases of the moon.

The moon goes through changes in appearance that we call 1. _phases_ . Because the moon produces no 2. _light_ of its own, we can only see what is reflected off of it from the 3. _sun_ . Half of the moon is always lit by the sun, but sometimes we see only a part of that. Half of the moon always 4. _faces_ us, but sometimes that includes an unlit part of the moon.

sun
faces
phases
light

5. **The Moon Phases***

Crescent Moon

Last Quarter

Gibbous

sunrays

Earth

New Moon

Full Moon

crescent

Gibbous

First Quarter

* Crescent – appears as a thin crescent

Gibbous – means swollen on one side or humpbacked

14

D. Solve the riddles with the help of the diagrams.

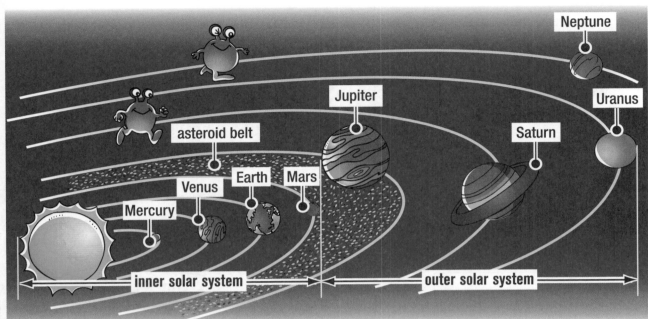

rocky   gas

1.

It's a natural satellite belonging to Earth. It has no water or air.

_____moon_____

2. It is the third planet from the sun. Its surface is mostly water.   _____Earth_____

3. The last of the gas giants, it was named for the God of the Sea.   _____Neptune_____

4. It looks spectacular, but it's just a dirty ball of ice.

comet

5. It is a rocky inner planet. It appears reddish from Earth because of the iron oxide in its soil.

Mars

6. It is small and orbits the sun with many others like it.

asteroid

7. Orbiting between Saturn and Neptune, its axis is such that it appears to be lying down.

Uranus

8. It is the closest planet to the sun. It is much smaller than Earth and has no moons.

Mercury

9. Unlike most of the others, it rotates east to west. It is the hottest, and often mistaken for a bright white star.

Venus

10.
> It's the largest planet, made mostly of hydrogen and helium. It has many moons.

Jupiter

11.
> Of all the gas planets, it's known for its rings. The others also have some, but it has the most.

Saturn

14

Planet Fun

It's easy to memorize the order of the planets from the sun! Make up a sentence with each word beginning with the first letter of each of the planets. It may be serious or silly. Look at my sentence.

Mercury
Venus
Earth
Mars
Jupiter
Saturn
Uranus
Neptune

Mr. Vampire Enjoys Magic
Juice So Unbearably Nasty

Your sentence:

_____

_____

Are you able to...

☐ tell the relationship between the Earth and the sun?

☐ identify the phases of the moon?

☐ describe the physical characteristics of the planets in our solar system?

☐ Use correct words to describe some objects in space?

The Night Sky

Dave, don't you know that northern lights is a common name for aurora borealis? They are only visible in the sky of the northern hemisphere.

In this unit, students will:

- identify, name, and describe night objects.
- name some constellations.
- label the Big Dipper, the Little Dipper, and Polaris and show the direction of north.

15

A. **Match the names with the pictures of the night objects. Then match the descriptions with the pictures. Write the letters.**

northern lights	constellation	meteoroid
comet	Milky Way	planet	moon

1.

moon — F

2.

meteoroid — D

3.

Milky Way — C

4.

constellation — A

5.

comet — B

6.

n o r t h e r n l i g h t s

G

Did you know that stars are spheres of hot gases?

7.

p l a n e t

E

Descriptions:

A Constellation
It is a group of stars that, as seen from the Earth, seems to form a picture.

B Comet
It is believed to be a mixture of ice, rock, and gas from a distance outside the solar system. It orbits the sun and has a distinct tail.

C Milky Way
Looking like milk spilled across the night sky, this is the galaxy we are a part of.

D Meteoroid
It is sometimes called a "shooting star" because that's what this broken bit of rock looks like when it enters the Earth's atmosphere.

E Planet eg Earth
It may look like a star in the sky, but this sunlight reflector doesn't twinkle unless it is near the horizon.

F Moon
This is, so far, the only celestial body humankind has set foot on.

G Northern Lights
Like a colourful light show, they are caused by particles from the sun mixing with gases in the Earth's upper atmosphere.

15

B. **Read what Doris says. Look at the star map. Then name the constellations.**

Groups of stars as seen from the Earth form patterns called constellations. The sky was mapped thousands of years ago, by different civilizations, into groups of stars that take the form of animals or mythical figures. These constellations are still in use today.

1. Pegasus

2. Cygnus

3. Leo

4. Cassiopeia

5. Draco

6. Orion

C. Read what Boris says. Connect the stars that form the Big Dipper and the Little Dipper and label them. Then circle Polaris and draw a line with a red pen from the man to show which direction is north.

If there were a line going through the Earth's axis and coming out of the North Pole, it would point directly at the star Polaris, also called the North Star. Because of this, Polaris is the only star in the sky that's always in the same place from anywhere we look, so it can be used for navigation purposes. You can see that Polaris is at the end of the handle of Little Dipper. When you find the Big Dipper, sight along the two stars at the end of the bowl of the Big Dipper, and Polaris is almost in line with those two stars.

North Star

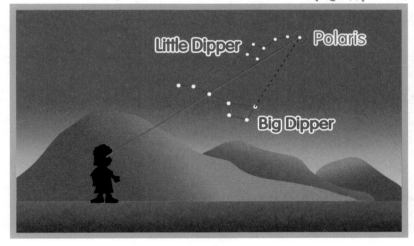

1.

2.

15

A Yummy Ice Cream Comet

Comets are made of ice, dust, and gas. Try this activity to make some "ice cream comets" and share them with your friends or family.

Materials:

- 1 tablespoon of sugar
- 125 mL of milk
- a few drops of vanilla oil
- 10 teaspoons of table salt
- 1 big and 1 small zipper bags
- some ice cubes
- crushed cookies or candies

Comet vs. Ice Cream Comet

frozen water = frozen milk

dust = crushed cookies

zipper bag

Steps:

1. Mix the milk, sugar, and vanilla oil in the small zipper bag and zip it.

2. Fill the big zipper bag half-full with ice cubes and add the salt.

3. Put the small bag into the big bag and zip the big bag.

4. Shake the big bag for about 5 minutes.

5. Squeeze the big bag gently and feel the mixture in the small bag to see whether it is hard or not. If it is, it is done; otherwise, shake more.

6. When it is ready, remove the small bag from the ice and rinse off the salt water from the small bag.

7. Open the small bag, add crushed cookies or candies, and enjoy!

Are you able to...

- [ ] identify, name, and describe night objects?
- [ ] name some constellations?
- [ ] label the Big Dipper, the Little Dipper, and Polaris and show the direction of north?

Find out more about the night sky on pages 118 and 119.

A. Complete the crossword puzzle.

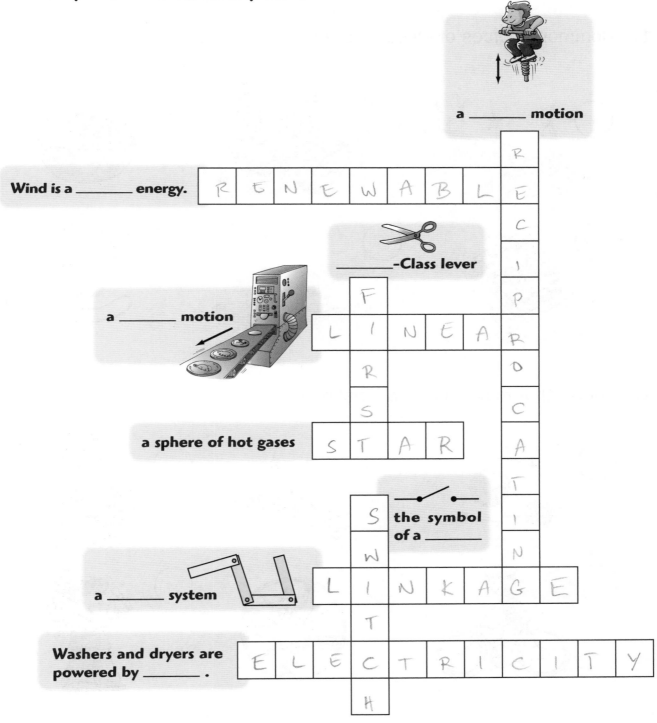

a _____ motion

Wind is a _____ energy. `R E N E W A B L E`

_____-Class lever

a _____ motion

a sphere of hot gases `S T A R`

the symbol of a _____

a _____ system `L I N K A G E`

Washers and dryers are powered by _____ . `E L E C T R I C I T Y`

Down word: `R E C I P R O C A T I N G`

`F L I N E A R S` (linear)

`S W I T C H` (switch)

electricity   first   linear   linkage

reciprocating   renewable   switch   star

B. Check the correct answers.

1. Common sources of electric power:

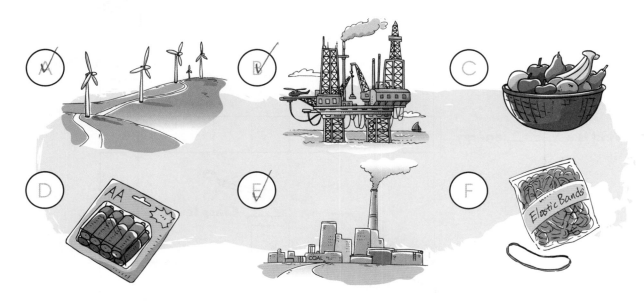

2. Things that move in a rotational motion:

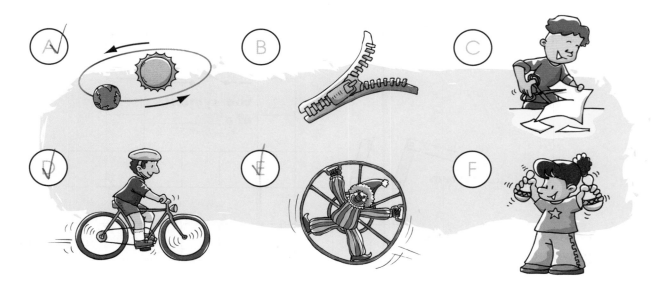

3. Planets:

4. The night object in the picture:

(A) northern lights

(B) moon

(C) constellations

(✓) Milky Way

5. Renewable sources of electric power:

(A) oil rig

(B) nuclear power generator

(✓) wind farm

(D) coal power generator

(✓) solar panels

(✓) hydroelectric dam

6. Examples of Second-Class Lever:

(A)

(✓B)

(✓C)

(D)

(✓E)

(F)

C. **Read the descriptions. Label the solar system with the words in bold.**

Jupiter : the largest planet in the solar system

Earth : the third planet from the sun

Mercury : the closest planet to the sun

Mars : a rocky inner planet, appears reddish from Earth because of the iron oxide in its soil

Saturn : with lots of rings

Neptune : the last of the gas giants, named for the God of the Sea

Uranus : in orbit between Saturn and Neptune

Venus : the second planet from the sun

asteroid belt : between the inner and outer solar systems

inner solar system : consists of the sun and four rocky planets

outer solar system : consists of four gaseous planets

Solar System

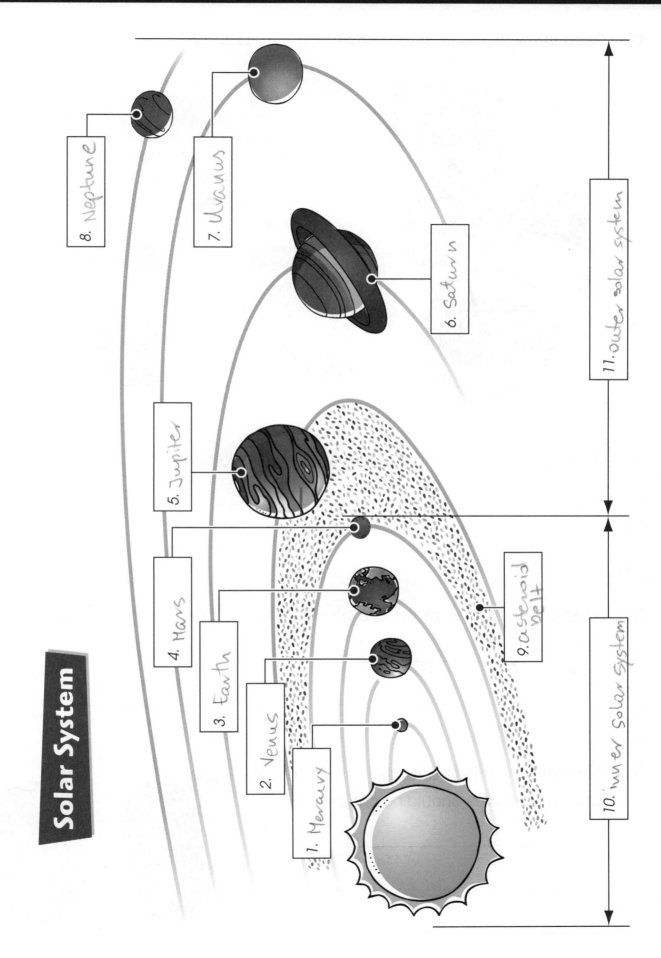

1. Mercury
2. Venus
3. Earth
4. Mars
5. Jupiter
6. Saturn
7. Uranus
8. Neptune
9. asteroid belt
10. inner Solar System
11. outer solar system

D. Read what Brandon says. Answer the questions.

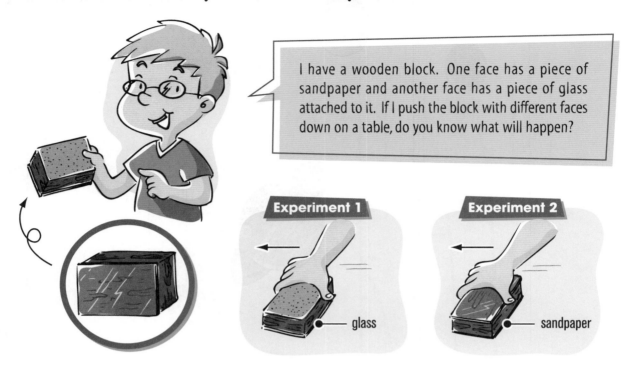

I have a wooden block. One face has a piece of sandpaper and another face has a piece of glass attached to it. If I push the block with different faces down on a table, do you know what will happen?

Experiment 1 — glass

Experiment 2 — sandpaper

1. On which face doesn't the block move easily? Why does this happen?

   _____

   _____

2. What can we do to make the block with that face down move faster?

   _____

   _____

3. If Mr. Smith wants to drive safer in winter time, which type of tires should he choose? Explain.

   _____

   _____

   _____

Fun & Useful Facts

Classification of Vertebrates

Animals belong to the animal kingdom. Scientists divide animals into two groups – invertebrates and vertebrates. Vertebrates are animals with backbones. They are grouped into five classes based on their skin covering, how they maintain body temperature, and characteristics of their limbs.

There are four kinds of reptiles: snakes and lizards, the crocodile family, tortoises and turtles, and the tuatara.

- cold-blooded
- have scales
- dry skin
- usually lay eggs, sometimes give birth to live young

Reptiles

Turtles have been on the Earth for more than 200 million years. They evolved before mammals, birds, crocodiles, snakes, and even lizards. Several species of turtles, including the American Box Turtle, can live to be over a hundred years of age.

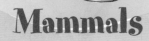

Mammals

- warm-blooded
- give birth to live young
- have hair or fur
- mothers nurse their young with milk

There are about 4500 different kinds of mammals. Most have babies that grow inside a mother's body. Bats are the only flying mammals.

Giant Pandas are on the endangered species list. The Chinese government has taken steps to protect these cute and adorable animals.

Penguins are birds, but they cannot fly. Emperor penguins are the largest of all the penguins.

- warm-blooded
- lay eggs
- have feathers and wings

There are more than 9000 kinds of birds. The largest groups are the passerines, or perching or song birds, like the robin. Hummingbirds are the only birds that are able to fly backward.

Birds

- cold-blooded
- covered with scales
- have fins
- lay many eggs
- breathe underwater using gills

There are more than 20 000 kinds of fish in the world. The earliest fossils of fish date back over 400 million years.

Fish

Many shark species are endangered. Fortunately, the Shark Foundation actively protects and researches endangered shark species and preserves their natural habitats.

More than 350 million years ago, fish-like amphibians moved onto land. Before dinosaurs came along, frogs, toads, salamanders, and newts had already been around for 150 million years.

Amphibians

- cold-blooded
- lay eggs
- moist, smooth skin
- webbed feet
- live on land and in water

There are three types of amphibians: frogs and toads, newts and salamanders, and caecilians. There are more than 4000 kinds of amphibians. Most amphibians change their appearance completely as they grow. This is called metamorphosis.

Electricity

There are two kinds of electricity – static electricity and current electricity.

Static electricity is a form of electricity that is created when an object has too many electrons, giving it a negative charge. Lightning is an example of static electricity.

Current electricity has a constant flow of electrons. A generator is used to convert the mechanical energy of a spinning turbine shaft into electrical energy through the use of magnetic fields. Electricity is then produced. A circuit is a path that electricity goes through. A closed circuit is a pathway of conductors through which an electric current flows. If any part of the circuit is removed or disconnected, the circuit is open which does not allow the flow of electricity.

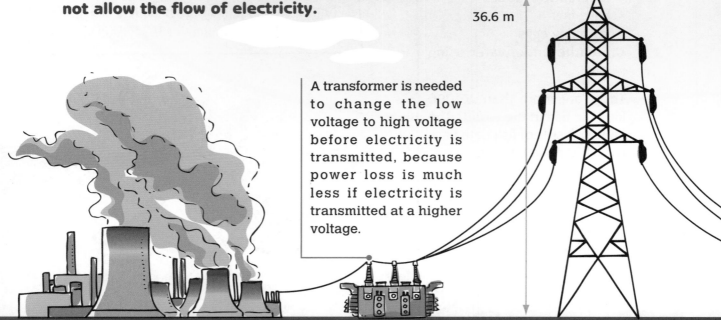

36.6 m

A transformer is needed to change the low voltage to high voltage before electricity is transmitted, because power loss is much less if electricity is transmitted at a higher voltage.

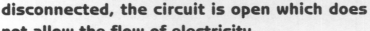

Power Plants　　　　**Transformer**

Power plants produce electricity on a large scale for industry, cities, and homes. They use giant generators, usually powered by gas, coal, oil, or the energy from nuclear reactions. Steam is produced at great pressure to drive a giant wheel called turbine to spin the coils of wire. The spinning turbine makes electricity. The electricity is transferred from the power plants to wherever it is needed through transmission lines.

Lightning occurs when the negative charges from the cloud meet positive charges rising from the ground.

A Flash of Lightning

Lightning happens when positive and negative charges move towards each other through the air. They make an electric current that causes a spark. This spark is the flash of lightning we see during a storm.

The CN Tower has a lightning rod. It is estimated that lightning strikes the CN Tower an average of 75 times a year.

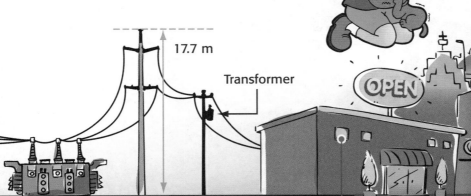

17.7 m

Transformer

o Transformer **Power Pole**

In order for your home to use electricity, it has to be at a lower voltage than on the transmission lines, so the voltage is much reduced by this transformer.

Electricity only flows if the circuit is closed. We use a switch to help us control the flow of electric current to the electrical device.

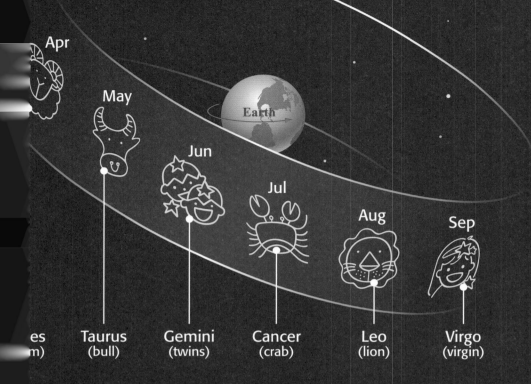

Apr

May

Jun

Jul

Aug

Sep

Earth

es
m)

Taurus
(bull)

Gemini
(twins)

Cancer
(crab)

Leo
(lion)

Virgo
(virgin)

Night Sky

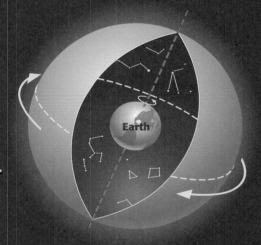

The Celestial Sphere

Earth

Ancient astronomers believed that the Earth is inside a dark sphere. They called it the "celestial sphere". They thought that the stars were struck on the inside of the sphere. When the sphere rotated, it made the stars move across the sky during the night. However, the movement of the stars is actually caused by the Earth's revolution. It makes the stars appear to travel across the sky.

A long time ago, astronomers made rough maps of the patterns that the brightest stars made. They also observed the sun, the moon, and the planets as they moved across a narrow band of stars. They believed that these stars somehow affected their lives. They divided the band into 12 constellations, with each of them representing a sign of the zodiac. Even today, some people still believe the stars affect their lives and this idea is called astrology.

Did you know that many of the constellations seen in the northern hemisphere are also seen in the southern hemisphere in the same month of the year? But they are seen in a different part of the sky and the star patterns seen on one side of the Earth are "upside-down" when viewed on the other side.

Because the Earth rotates counterclockwise, it makes the stars appear to travel in a clockwise direction.

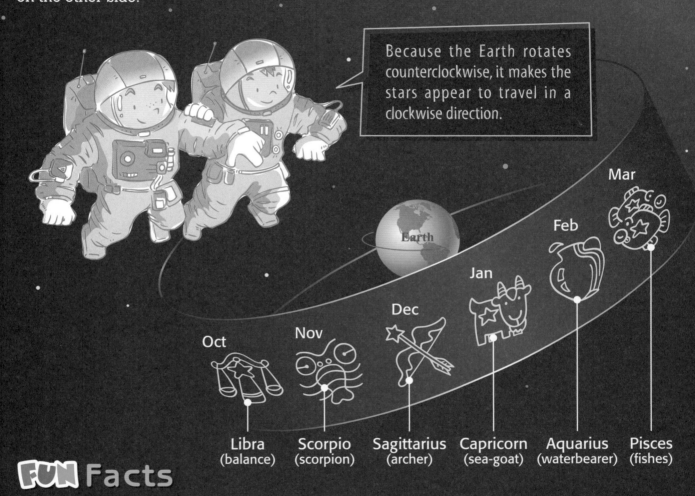

Mar

Feb

Jan

Dec

Nov

Oct

Libra
(balance)

Scorpio
(scorpion)

Sagittarius
(archer)

Capricorn
(sea-goat)

Aquarius
(waterbearer)

Pisces
(fishes)

FUN Facts

- Stars are balls of hot gases. The inside of a star is its hottest part, which is 60 000 times hotter than the hottest oven.

- Stars have different colours. The hottest stars are blue, the coldest ones are red, and yellow ones are in between.

- The sun is a star that gives us the light and heat that we need to survive.

- We have named 88 constellations (constellation means a group of stars that seems to form a pattern or picture) so far.

Questions & Answers

1. Which constellation can be seen in the southern hemisphere only?

2. Which star stands almost motionless in the northern sky?

Answers: 1. Crux (the Southern Cross)
2. Polaris

Answers

1   Classification

A.

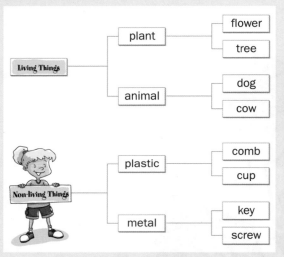

B. 1. organisms   2. structures
    3. invertebrates   4. vertebrates
    5. Vertebrate: cat ; turtle ; shark ; snake ; bird ; cheetah
        Invertebrate: snail ; squid ; centipede ; grasshopper ; earthworm ; jellyfish
C. temperature ; cold-blooded ; warm-blooded
    1. warm-blooded   2. warm-blooded
    3. cold-blooded   4. warm-blooded
    5. cold-blooded   6. warm-blooded
    7. cold-blooded

D.

a	b	a	r	e	p	t	i	l	e	s	m	n	k	j
c	t	m	a	m	m	a	l	s	x	p	o	b	e	x
e	w	p	q	t			t	o	d	m	i	l	k	
n	a	h	y	n			h	s	f	o	r	a	u	
t	f	i	s	h	s	z	f	o	k	s	l	d	d	d
i	t	b	g	o	p	u	r	r	e	y	l	s	g	m
p	s	i	x	u	o	p	w	a	l	k	u	h	a	s
e	s	a		n	e	y	x	e	a	s	g	l	g	
d	w	n		g	z	n	a	t	h	k	i	i		
e	j	s	b	o	e		o	f	s	l		l		
s	w	o	r	m	s			n	w	j	l	v	r	
				i	n	s	e	c	t	s	n	w		
m	i	l	q	a	r	t	h	r	o	p	o	d	a	d

Try this!
Activity

2   Invertebrates

A. 1. arthropods   2. sand dollars
    3. worms   4. sponges
    5. sea anemones   6. mollusks

B. 1. worms ; F
    2. arthropods ; B
    3. mollusks ; C
    4. sand dollars ; A
    5. sponges ; E
    6. sea anemones ; D

C. 1. arthropods   2. adaptations
    3. exoskeleton   4. sense
    5. sound   6. three
    7. thorax   8. legs
    9. circulation
    10.    11.
    12.

D. 1. insects   2. sense organs
    3. dragonfly   4. legs
    5. exoskeleton   6. three
    7. thorax   8. arthropod

Try this!
(Individual observation)

3   Vertebrates (1)

A. 1. Carolus Linnaeus
    2. There are seven levels of classification, which are kingdom, phylum, class, order, family, genus, and species.
    3. They put organisms into groups based on their body structures.
    4. Yes, because both left and right parts of vertebrates' bodies are the same.

B. 1. Fish ; shark
    2. Amphibian ; bullfrog
    3. Bird ; ostrich
    4. Reptile ; crocodile
    5. Mammal ; human being

C. 1. Skin   2. barrier
    3. organs   4. camouflage

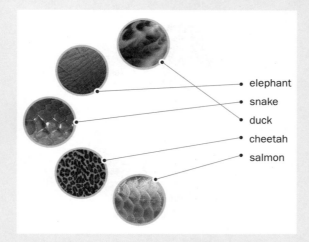

D.   (Individual answers)

Try this!
      Activity

4   Vertebrates (2)

A.   1.   adaptations
      2.   eat
      3.   animals
      4.   E ; D ; C ; F ; A ; B
B.   (Suggested answer for each example)
      1.   F ; lion   2.   D ; horse
      3.   A ; crocodile   4.   C ; nectar-eating bat
      5.   E ; whale shark   6.   B ; lizard
C.   1.   reproduce   2.   life
      3.   offspring   4.   one
      5.   (Suggested answers)
            one or a few offspring at a time:
            elephant ; monkey
            many offspring at a time:
            mouse ; frog
D.   1.   African elephant ; Yes
      2.   Wood frog ; No
      3.   Sea turtle ; No
      4.   Great blue heron ; Yes
      5.   If a parent reproduces only one or a few
            offspring at a time, it invests time and energy
            in the upbringing.

Try this!
      (Individual research)

5   Properties of Air (1)

A.   Evidence of Air:
      bubble filled with air ; chimney smoke blown
      sideways ; kite in air ; balloon filled with air ; fan
      induces moving air ; pinwheel moving ; candle flame
      being blown out ; wind blowing hat off ; basketball
      filled with air

B.   1.   air
      2.   weight
      3.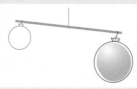

      4.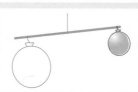

      5.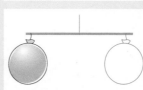

      6.   heavier
C.   1.   The warm water heats the air inside the bottle
            and the air expands to fill the balloon.
      2.   The air inside the balloon cools and
            compresses. The balloon is deflated again.
      3.   expands ; lighter
D.   Steps: 2 ; 1 ; 3
      expands ; heated
E.   1.   rises   2.   on
      3.   warm   4.   bottom

Try this!
      Air

Review 1

A.

				W					R	
V	E	R	T	E	B	R	A	T	E	S
				I					P	
		L	E	G	S				T	
				H					I	
				T					L	
									E	
	M	A	M	M	A	L	S		S	
			O							
			L							
E	X	O	S	K	E	L	E	T	O	N
			U							
			S							
		S	K	I	N					
			S							

ANSWERS

B. 1. A ; C ; D ; E ; F
    2. A ; C ; E
    3. A ; D
    4. A ; D
    5. B ; C
    6. A ; C
    7. B ; C
C. 1. E   2. C
    3. B   4. D
    5. A
D. (Individual drawings)
    1. Reptile   2. Bird
    3. Fish   4. Amphibian
    5. Mammal
E. **Experiment 1:**
    The air inside the ball expands.
    Experiment 2:
    The air inside the poked balloon is leaking from the hole and the balloon becomes lighter.

6 Properties of Air (2)

A. dry ; air ; space
    The air will leave the glass and water will enter to take its space. The tissue will be wet.
B. 1. B   2. A ; C
C. 1. compressed 2. insulator
    3. more   4. conserve
    5. Compressibility: B ; D ; E
        Insulating quality: A ; C ; F
D. 1. A   2. E
    3. F   4. D
    5. G   6. B
    7. C

Try this!
    Activity

7 Characteristics of Flight (1)

A. 1. lift   2. Bernoulli
    3. lower   4. higher
    5. lift   6. lower
    7. slower
B. 1.

    decrease ; down

2.

    less ; higher ; rise

C. 1. lift   2. airfoil
    3. below   4. faster
    5. B ; D ; E
D. 1. E   2. D
    3. C   4. F
    5. A   6. B

Try this!
Activity

8 Characteristics of Flight (2)

A. 1. drag   2. increased
    3. balanced
    4.   5.

    6.

B. 1. streamlined ; drag ; air
    2. B
    3. B
    4. C
C. 1.

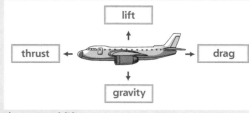

    2. Thrust and lift
    3. Lift and gravity
D. 1. drag   2. streamlined
    3. Bernoulli   4. thrust
    5. lift   6. dragonfly

Try this!

The balloon goes to the other end of the string. As the air inside the balloon escapes the opening of the balloon, it creates thrust, the force that propels the balloon to the other end of the string.

9 Static and Current Electricity (1)

A. (Suggested answer for each example)
 1. lamp ; laptop computer ; telephone ; printer ; digital clock ; photocopier ; **calculator**
 2. refrigerator ; oven ; microwave ; range hood ; stove ; coffee maker ; **toaster**

B. 1. Static 2. rubbed
 3. Current 4. heat
 5. static electricity 6. current electricity
 7. static electricity 8. current electricity

C. 1. conductor ; insulator
 2. Conductor: juice ; toonie ; fork
 Insulator: eraser ; ball ; book
 3a. insulator b. conductor
 c. insulator d. conductor

D. 1.  2. closed circuit

 3. closed circuit 4.

 5.  6. closed circuit

Try this!

Experiment 1:
The two balloons move away from each other.
Experiment 2:
The two balloons move away from each other.
Experiment 3:
The two balloons move close together.
When the balloons are rubbed by the same material, they will carry the same electrical charge to make them move apart. When the balloons are rubbed by different materials, one will become positively charged and the other will become negatively charged. Therefore, they attract each other.

10 Static and Current Electricity (2)

A. 1. cell 2. switch
 3. bulb 4. wire

B. 1. 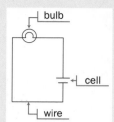 2.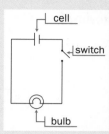

C. 1.
 2. CC
 3. CC
 4.
 5.
 6. CC

D. 1. series
 2. parallel
 3. series
 4. parallel
 5. series
 6. parallel

E. 1. Series Circuit: A ; D
 Parallel Circuit: B ; C
 2. The pathway would be broken and the current of electricity would be unable to flow. The other light bulb would not operate.
 3. The pathway to the other light bulb would remain open to the flow of electricity. The other light bulb would still operate.

Try this!

(Individual observation)

ANSWERS

Review 2

A.

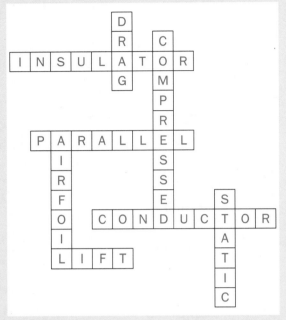

B.
1. A ; E ; F
2. B
3. B ; C ; D ; F
4. A ; B
5. A ; D
6. B ; D

C.
1. Air resists things flowing through it.
2. Air expands when heated.
3. Air occupies space.
4. Air has insulating quality.

D.
1. A.

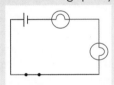

    B.

    C.

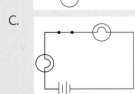

2. A and C
3. The pathway will be broken. The current of electricity will not be able to flow and the other bulb will not operate.

E.

decreases ; down

F.
1.

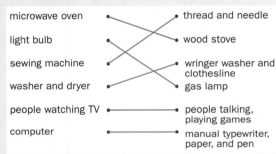

2. thrust

11   More about Electricity

A.   B ; C ; F

B.
1.

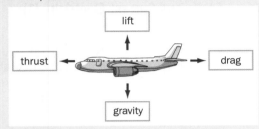

2. (Individual answer)

C.
1. hydroelectric dam
2. solar panels
3. wind farm
4. oil rig
5. coal power generator
6. nuclear power generator
7. solar panels ; renewable
8. oil rig ; non-renewable
9. nuclear power generator ; non-renewable
10. coal power generator ; non-renewable
11. hydroelectric dam ; renewable
12. wind farm ; renewable

Try this!
Activity

12   Motion

A.
1. reciprocating ; straight line
2. rotational ; circular path
3. linear ; one direction
4. oscillating ; back-and-forth

B. Trace the dotted lines.
1. reciprocating
2. reciprocating motion
3. rotational motion
4. reciprocating motion
5. oscillating motion
6. rotational motion

C. 1. reduce ; A
2. increase ; B
3. increase ; B
4. reduce ; A
5. reduce ; A

Try this!
Observation:
The elastic band stretches out more with the block on the sandpaper.
Explanation:
The friction on the sandpaper is greater than that on the table. We need more effort to overcome the friction when the block is being pulled.

13   Motion and Machines

A. 1. A. screw
B. wheel and axle
C. wedge
D. inclined plane
E. lever
2. pulley
3. screw
4. wedge
5. The machines that use rotational motion are screw, pulley, and wheel and axle.

B. First-Class Lever:

effort ;

Second-Class Lever:

effort ;

Third-Class Lever:

fulcrum ;

C. (Individual design)

D. Trace the arrows.
1. An extra tray is unfolded.
2. The hand of the clown stretches out.

Try this!
Activity

14   Earth and Our Solar System

A. 1. axis
2. day
3. year
4. orbit
5. northern
6. southern

B. Moon

C. 1. phases
2. light
3. sun
4. faces
5.

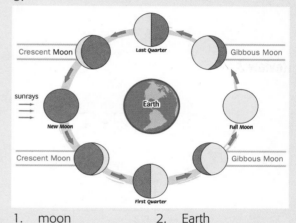

D. 1. moon
2. Earth
3. Neptune
4. comet
5. Mars
6. asteroid
7. Uranus
8. Mercury
9. Venus
10. Jupiter
11. Saturn

Try this!
Activity

15   The Night Sky

A. 1. moon ; F
2. meteoroid ; D
3. Milky Way ; C
4. constellation ; A
5. comet ; B
6. northern lights ; G
7. planet ; E

B. 1. Pegasus
2. Cygnus
3. Leo
4. Cassiopeia
5. Draco
6. Orion

C. 1.

2.

Try this!
  Activity

Review 3

A.

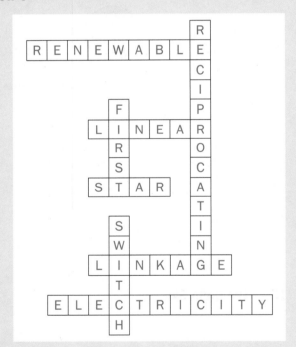

B. 1. A ; B ; E
   2. A ; D ; E
   3. A ; B ; F
   4. D
   5. C ; E ; F
   6. B ; C ; E

C. 1. Mercury
   2. Venus
   3. Earth
   4. Mars
   5. Jupiter
   6. Saturn
   7. Uranus
   8. Neptune
   9. asteroid belt
   10. inner solar system
   11. outer solar system

D. 1. The block with the sandpaper does not move easily because it has greater friction than the block with the glass.
   2. We can decrease the friction by adding water or oil on the table.
   3. He should choose A because more treads on the tires create greater friction on the icy and slippery road in winter time.